THE STUDY OF POLITICS

The Present State of American Political Science

University of Illinois Press, Urbana, 1959

Charles S. Hyneman

THE STUDY OF
POLITICS

THE PRESENT STATE OF AMERICAN POLITICAL SCIENCE

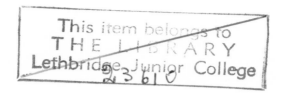
SECOND PRINTING, 1961; THIRD PRINTING, 1963

© 1959 by the Board of Trustees of the University of Illinois.
Library of Congress Catalog Card No. 59-10554.
Manufactured in the United States of America.

To

JEAN DRISCOLL AND LAWRENCE HERSON
*because they worked persistently and
patiently at my education*

PREFACE

This essay is addressed to graduate students. My aim is to tell young men and young women some things it may be good to know about the profession they intend to enter. If old timers think they learn something also, they are welcome to whatever they pick up.

If many older members of the profession read this, some of them will find confirmation of their own positions. They may even encounter some of their own ideas stated in their own words. For I have freely utilized what I have heard said over a period of at least three decades. I hope, of course, that I have myself added something to the discussion. If I have, it is not likely to sound new to men of my own age. I have not won any prizes for keeping my thoughts to myself over the years. But the young people, I have hope, will encounter a thing or two here they have not already pondered.

The pages which follow present only a small part of what I think young people ought to be told about their discipline and profession. The reason for offering this partial statement at this time is this. During the last years of my tenure at Northwestern University, the faculty in political science was very generously encouraged by the Carnegie Corporation to examine the problems of study and teaching in political science with a view to revision of its own curriculum and study program. In the last year of that period I was freed from a part of my teaching duties to set forth my own views about the status of political science in the United States. The scope of my inquiry and the character of my analysis were largely determined by the expectation that my essay would be the first part of a substantial volume, my statement to be followed by essays in which some other members of the department examined various challenges confronting political scientists and opportunities available to them. These hopes did not materialize, and I am happy that this fragment is thought worthy of publication by itself.

Anyone who writes thoughtfully about his profession is bound to be a parasite on innumerable and often unremembered colleagues. The bibliography lists those who have written most directly about academic study of government and politics, but I must have omitted items which contributed importantly to my beliefs and my evaluations. I think it proper to say that I did not see Dwight Waldo's UNESCO study until my own essay was in its present form except for references to most recent literature. If Waldo's shrewd observations had been available earlier, many of my own statements might have been different.

Of my teachers, Frank G. Bates undoubtedly did most to put my intellectual house in order and prepare me for the serious study of government and politics. Of my faculty associates, Charles M. Kneier did more than any other to knock sense into my head. Of my friends and talking companions for twenty years or more, Willmoore Kendall, Evron Kirkpatrick, and Harold Stoke undoubtedly did more than any others to clutter up my mind and then kindly clear it up again. If they like what I say here, they can share credit; if they don't like it, they can vote to put one of themselves in the doghouse.

While this essay is wholly my own and not institutionally

endorsed, I must pay tribute to a number of associates at Northwestern University who encouraged this enterprise, helped me get my thoughts in order, and moved burdens from my shoulders to their own. William McGovern, Roland Young, Kathleen Young, and my wife gave aid and comfort that cannot be identified here. Robert Browning of the Philosophy Department looked after my education for nearly ten years. Richard Snyder showed me how to improve this essay at several points. David Apter was most generous in challenging my suppositions and convictions, just as generous in supplying replacements for the props he knocked from under me. But more than to any of these, I am indebted to a sizable number of graduate students and beginning teachers who gratified my ego by listening patiently, but who also found uncountable opportunities to throw me off my track and set me on a better one. I cannot name all of them. The rest will forgive me for acknowledging special debt to Sidney Baldwin, David Derge, Charles Gilbert, Philip Haring, Milton Hobbs, James Murray, and Karl O'Lessker. Two others I make a special place for on another page.

Finally, I thank James A. Robinson who examined and reported on several items of literature at my request, and Byrum Carter, Charles Hagan, Jeane Kirkpatrick, Austin Ranney, Jack W. Peltason, and Mulford Sibley, who read parts or all of this essay in manuscript and convinced me that I should make several changes.

CHARLES S. HYNEMAN

CONTENTS

part I

POLITICAL SCIENCE:
THE GRAND ENTERPRISE

CHAPTER I

The Preoccupations of American Political Scientists

This inquiry into the present state of political science and the problems confronting members of the profession originated in a belief that political scientists throughout the country are unhappy about the state of their discipline. The apprehension which underlies present dissatisfaction with political science and which stimulates debate about what we ought to be doing seems to be rooted in four sources of doubt and fear: (1) Fear that we engage too much in activities which divert us from scholarly study and adversely affect the quality of the studies we make; (2) Fear that we have set ourselves too great a task in scholarly study; that we have committed ourselves to objectives of inquiry which in magnitude and diversity are too great to be encompassed in a discipline; (3) Doubt that our scholarly enterprise promises to achieve results worthy of a place in the total structure of learned literature; (4) Doubt that we have fitted our efforts adequately with the efforts of other disciplines that share with us the whole study of social relationships.

An examination of these sources of doubt and fear requires us to take note of the activities that compete with scholarly study for our attention, to assess the magnitude and diversity of our objectives in study, to face up to conflict that divides us in respect to goals and methods of study, and to give attention to some choices which are available to us in the further development of our literature and in the training of political scientists who will succeed us. What I have to say about these matters seems logically to fall into three parts: Part I, a single chapter which briefly identifies the major preoccupations (or whole enterprise) of the profession; Part II, five chapters which attempt to describe the scholarly undertaking of American political scientists; and Part III, five chapters which attempt to identify, and I hope illuminate in some measure, the issues on which political scientists divide in evaluating their contributions to scholarship.

I have purposefully kept the descriptive statements short and limited analysis to the main points requiring attention. What I say is designed to excite and suggest, not to persuade or convince. There are no recommendations for increase of effort, reallocation of emphasis, or change of course. I think it best to confine this essay to diagnosis and leave prescription to other persons or other times.

THE SEVERAL CONCERNS OF THE POLITICAL SCIENTISTS

Observation of what American political scientists are doing and have been doing in recent years indicates that they engage in four kinds of enterprise. (1) They carry on scholarly study and pass on the fruits of their study in writings and teaching. (2) They give advice on current issues of public policy and participate in the formation and execution of public policy. (3) They train men and women for public service. And (4), a recent innovation, they carry on activities in foreign countries directed toward education and training of people and improvement of government and political practices.

Scholarship the Primary Task

It will readily be agreed that scholarship—which includes study, publication, and teaching—is the primary task of the political scientist. It is primary because it contributes more to the other activities of political scientists than those other activities contribute to scholarship. Participation in public affairs informs the student and may provide him with understanding which redirects his scholarly effort. But scholarly study can be carried on effectively by political scientists who remain aloof from the public forum. The reverse is not true, however; the political scientist cannot take expertise as a political scientist to the public forum except as he carries with him the fruits of scholarship. He may personally refuse to engage in studious inquiry, even ignore the literature which others have produced, and participate effectively in public affairs as a citizen. But in this case his contributions are comparable to those of other citizens. In this case he does not bring to public policy and governmental activity the special gifts of a learned discipline.

A conviction that scholarship is the first obligation of the profession gives one a basis for evaluating the other preoccupations of political scientists. If other preoccupations are found to support and enrich the scholarly undertaking, they pass a high test of worthiness. If they are found only to be special outlets for the knowledge accumulated by the profession, neither contributing to nor setting obstacles to further study, one may view such activities with approval up to the point where indulgence in them is thought excessive because it too greatly diverts effort from the scholarly enterprise. But if the other preoccupations, or any part of them, are thought injurious to scholarship, adversely affecting the amount and quality of serious study, for instance, it may be concluded that the social gains derived from these other preoccupations notably fail to balance the losses sustained from the impairment of scholarship.

Participation in Public Affairs

It may be that no student of political science can escape some measure of participation in public affairs. All of us talk to others about issues of public policy and to that extent all of us help form public opinion and indirectly influence decisions. It may be that few (possibly none) of us evade a further stage of involvement—delivery of public addresses in which we analyze and evaluate existing and proposed arrangements, policies, and practices. It may even be the case that no political scientist can deny having personally advocated action which seemed to him in accord with public interest.

Participation which goes beyond talk is, of course, much less universally shared by members of the profession. Even so, we must count as major activities of American political scientists service as consultants to governments, employment in administrative and other governmental positions, involvement in political party activity and electoral campaigns, and occasional candidacies for elective public offices.

The foregoing types of participation represent individual enterprises. Ordinarily the individual political scientist decides for himself what he will do and when and how he will do what he does. But not always. Participation in public affairs is also institutionalized. It is sponsored by the institutions in which we are employed, and services may be required of some of us which we are reluctant to give. Many a young political scientist has unhappily accepted employment part time or whole time in a bureau of government research because he saw no hope of getting the teaching appointment he preferred. Many an older political scientist has directed bureau studies which he counted marginal to our long-run scholarly enterprise and which he undertook because people not of the discipline, in and out of the university, thought the university ought to render a special service to society. No doubt many studies by bureaus of government research, planned and executed by political scientists, are destined to become main items in an enduring literature of political science. Perhaps most of them add something of genuine significance to our scholarly product. It may be that all of them supply those who make the study with fuller understanding of matters political scientists want to study, and sharpen their appreciation of what we are up against in getting knowledge we want to acquire. Allowing each of these statements to represent the facts, we must still acknowledge that many political scientists believe that many bureau activities divert men of high competence for scholarship from great opportunities to marginal opportunities for contribution to an enduring literature.

Training for Public Service

All intellectual development is valuable training for public service. In providing part of a liberal arts education, political science departments contribute importantly to the preparation of young people for governmental employment. But the fact that government is the primary object of their study has led to public expectation that political scientists will do a great deal more than other liberal arts departments to give college students knowledge and points of view appropriate for careers in government service. Students press us to offer courses which look good on applications for public jobs. Individuals and groups to whom college and university officials are attentive urge the academic institution to do something to assure a more competent and more devoted governmental personnel, and officials of the institution drop the problem in the lap of the political science department.

We try to meet the problem in two ways. We add a few courses which provide special knowledge about living in and operating governmental organizations but which can also be counted as credit toward a liberal arts degree. Or we create a specialized curriculum which we call a Public Service

Training Program. Regardless of which step we take to meet the demand put upon us, we stir up intellectual conflict among ourselves. If we offer a course in personnel administration or fiscal administration for liberal arts credit, someone in the political science department argues (with support from people in other academic departments) that we have sold our intellectual birthright for a mess of vocational pottage. If we create a special curriculum in public service training, someone argues that the tail is certain to wag the dog because the institution cannot adequately finance both the specialized training and a vigorous program of scholarly study and liberal teaching of political science.

Training and Improvement Programs Abroad

Political scientists who view with alarm the attention given to public service training on the campus find additional cause for alarm when the university establishes an outpost in a foreign country. The University of Michigan establishes a center of administrative studies and a public service training program in the Philippines and staffs the operations mainly with political scientists. Michigan State University moves into Indo-China. Indiana University plants an installation in Thailand. Other American universities set up shop in other places. And in many of these new ventures political scientists direct the operations and constitute most of the staff of specialists.

These enterprises are defended as service which society may properly expect of a profession it maintains and as new fountains of experience which enrich scholarly study. They are deplored by others as diversions from the scholarly study some political scientists believe society needs more than it needs these new ventures. Dissatisfactions arising on this count cumulate with dissatisfactions arising out of extensive participation in public affairs and provision of special training for persons in the public service or planning to enter public service. We shall now take a quick look at the main lines of argument in the controversy which ensues.

INJURY, DIVERSION, OR ENRICHMENT?

Disagreements within the profession that can be related to choice among the four major preoccupations just identified may stem from issues of fact or from issues of evaluation. Argument may arise from different estimates of how American political scientists actually distribute their time and effort; or it may arise from different convictions about how political scientists ought to distribute their time and effort.

Differences of the first order need not occupy us here. Presumably they will evaporate when we assemble evidence as to what American political scientists have been and are now doing. But issues of the second order cannot be resolved by arrays of evidence which appear obtainable. The social gains attributable to particular activities, and the prices paid because men do those things instead of something else, are not readily established by research. Differences in judgment about what political scientists ought to be doing, and therefore whether they are at any time doing what a society ultimately will find most useful, are bound to persist and we shall be lucky if they are not a continuing source of unhappiness. Intellectual conflict which arises out of different evaluations of our several major preoccupations consequently is worthy of most careful attention.

Those members of the profession who are most unhappy about the present distribution of effort base their complaint on two grounds. They believe: (1) that certain major activities of American political scientists are incompatible with scholarly study; and (2) that certain other activities which may be helpful to scholarship if properly restrained have been carried to excess and are allowed to divert many of us from the primary task of scholarly study.

A composite of the specific charges reads like this. Some of us, at the drop of a hat or a ten-dollar bill, will tell a woman's club things that we would not try to defend before a group of professional colleagues. Some of us, for exaltation of ego or enlargement of family income, devote so much time to the public forum that none is left for making additions to scholarship. We seek and hold public positions as consultants, administrative employees, and elected officials, and some of us have been known to assert that attainment of such positions marks the highest achievement possible for political scientists. Many of us are so caught up in partisanship relating to contests for office or issues of public policy that objectivity in study and teaching is impaired; and some of us are involved as partisans to the point where we entirely lose capacity for objectivity, carry partisanship into the classroom and harangue or browbeat students, and let partisan commitments rather than a desire to advance understanding determine what we write about and how we develop our discourse. We honor studies which are designed wholly to implement contemporary public policy, producing no residue of knowledge that can enter into an enduring literature of political science; and study of this kind is institutionalized in bureaus of government research managed and staffed by political scientists. Furthermore, people who are employed in bureaus of government research have to report findings and recommendations before careful and comprehensive inquiry can be made. Protracted experience in such superficial study fixes habits and states of mind incompatible with high-quality research and analysis when these people get a chance to return to more leisurely scholarship. The presence in or near the political science department of a bureau consequently nourishes tolerance of careless workmanship among others because political scientists with high standards of scholarship see credit given for report writing and publications which at best meet low standards of scholarship and at worst propound deceit rather than knowledge.

Political scientists who reject this sweeping indictment respond to it in widely different fashions. Their responses vary according to differences of judgment on at least three matters.

First, judgments differ as to whether the facts are as alleged. As noted above, careful research has not established the facts as to how American political scientists distribute time and effort among their major preoccupations. Naturally, political scientists who believe that few of us carry any evidences of partisanship into our teaching and writing and that none of us are significantly prejudiced will wholly dismiss that item in the indictment.

Second, among those who admit that the facts are as alleged, judgments differ as to what kinds of study political scientists ought to be carrying on and as to what are the characteristics or marks of scholarly effort. Many political scientists believe the primary objective of study should be the provision of knowledge which has immediate usefulness to one or another of several publics—to men and women seeking fuller understanding of their government in order to adjust themselves more comfortably to its decrees or to participate more effectively in controlling it, to political leaders seeking fuller understanding of alternatives available to them in formation of public policy, to public officials and employees seeking fuller understanding of how they can most economically proceed to the realization of objectives they have before them. In striking contrast are many other political scientists who have a low regard for study which pays off quickly. This is the case with those who think our prime objective should be the creation of a science. Knowledge worthy of being called science ultimately provides guidance in establishing goals and devising means for achieving goals. But the men who produce the science are generally content to cumulate, order, and continuously restructure the body of knowledge and show little concern about when that body of knowledge begins to pay off in guidance of individual or social conduct. A gulf of like proportions separates one group of political scientists who think the first obligation of the profession is to help people critically examine their value holdings from another group who think the whole job of the political scientist is to understand and explain what actually exists and occurs in the world.

Men who differ so greatly in conviction about proper objectives of study and tests of scholarship are bound to differ greatly in the way they respond to charges that various activities in which they indulge divert members of the profession from scholarship or impair the quality of the study they undertake. If A thinks the prime goal in scholarship is a full description of governmental-political institutions and practices and the identification and explanation of alternatives available to people who do not like their governmental-political system, he may conclude that active participation in public affairs is an essential means for informing the scholar and a necessary outlet for the special knowledge which the scholar acquires. If, in contrast, B thinks the prime goal of scholarship is the establishment and interrelating of scientific propositions and C thinks the prime goal is imaginative contemplation of what men value most highly—for B and C the experience acquired by participation in public affairs may contribute only slightly to scholarship, or be irrelevant to scholarship, or even be injurious.

Third, among those who are of like mind as to what political scientists ought to study and what constitutes scholarly achievement there will be differences of judgment as to what effects the other preoccupations have on scholarship. One man thinks a certain kind of participation in public affairs excites men to undertake a serious study but another is sure that it diverts more men from serious study than it attracts. One man thinks that certain activities supply knowledge essential for accurate description and thoughtful analysis, but another thinks those experiences delude men, causing them to suppose that casual observation supplies knowledge which can only be obtained by more rigorous inquiry procedures. And so it goes.

Acknowledging that no single statement in rebuttal will satisfy more than a limited sector of the profession, we may propose an imagined response thought likely to express the views of those who most fully reject the bill of indictment set forth above. The defense will rest on two grounds. It will argue first that, rather than divert men from scholarship or depress the quality of study which is undertaken, the major preoccupations identified above excite men to undertake serious inquiry and enrich the quality of the literature they produce. And it will argue second that, regardless of their relation to the production of a scholarly literature, these preoccupations are imperatives for the profession because they are indispensable means for delivering the product of our scholarly effort to the society which maintains us.

Participation in public affairs, begins the statement in defense, excites men to scholarly enterprise and directs their attention to objects of attention most needful of exploration. One might wish that training for scholarly study guaranteed impulse and incentive to engage in scholarly study but the guarantee is not delivered with the certificate of entry to the profession. Close association with men of affairs and personal involvement in issues of public policy supply impetus and incentive to political scientists who lack a self-starter. These associations and involvements do more than whip up interest; they challenge the political scientist to evaluations. They challenge him to evaluate himself and to evaluate his environment. Arriving at a better appreciation of his own value holdings and a fuller understanding of social needs,

he puts the two together in the form of decisions to re-
examine suppositions and beliefs, seek further knowledge,
and pass on to others the results of careful and thoughtful
inquiry. And the process is infectious. The enthusiasm
aroused in this way rubs off on colleagues less inclined to
get out of the library, and the diligence displayed by those
who are so aroused shames inert colleagues into action. Even
the bureau of government research that responds most su-
pinely to deadlines and is least noted for quality of research
may set models for some other political scientists not plagued
by deadlines because they have not started anything which
they expect to finish.

By participation in public affairs, the defense continues,
we establish confidences with individuals and publics which
give us access to data that can be exploited in scholarly study.
Confidence and access are cumulative and expansive. The
political scientist who brings good will, reasonableness, and
special knowledge to one group struggling with a problem
wins confidence and access from still other people who have
only heard of his notable performance. The good reputation
of one man who is thought of as a political scientist opens
doors for another man who calls himself a political scientist.
The bureau of government research, by establishing a record
of helpful service, in effect grants passports which authorize
political scientists of that university to travel at will through
city halls, county courthouses, and establishments of the
state government.

Beyond this, participation informs men for scholarship.
Knowledge does not start with books; it starts with experience of living. If the proper study of mankind is man, the
proper way to study man is to be around man and observe
him. The finer differentiations in descriptions of what men
do and how they do it, and the nicer evaluations of data
which must be assimilated in judgments, can only be made
by men with sure knowledge. And sure knowledge is

acquired by observing men at critical moments and by experiencing personally the sentiments and the emotions which affect behavior but cannot be observed in behavior.

Scholarship is accordingly enriched by a due amount of participation in public affairs. Views about what are crucial problems for society are changed. False beliefs about what people want and what they will put up with are corrected. Understanding is improved as to when and where social decisions are made and who supplies support and who supplies resistance to proposed actions. These may be regarded as crude gains, directing the participant-student to new objects of study, informing him in design of research, and shortening his steps in acquisition of data. To these crude gains must be added the more precious ones cited above, items of sure knowledge which pay off in finer differentiations and nicer evaluations. Lacking the gains that come from a due participation in public affairs, we are in bondage to the literature that comes down to us and victims of the error it contains. Informed by participation, each of us has an independent base for belief and for judgment, and the discipline escapes the straitjacket that otherwise would have been imposed by common dependence on one body of literature.

The defense of the activities cited as competitors with scholarship rests also on society's immediate need for expertise. Political scientists, like members of all other learned disciplines, are maintained by society because someone expects them to deliver a service. We may prefer to operate on a long-term credit basis, promising society no returns on its investment, other than current teaching, until after we have matured our scholarship and developed a firm literature of dependable findings. But others, who speak for society, will share in the decision as to what our obligations are and when we should deliver on them. If people who provide the money we live on or the institutional officials who allocate the money among different groups of scholars (disciplines) conclude that political scientists are not worth much now and may be a poor bet for the future, we may find our salaries stationary when salaries of others go up, or see our numbers decline as professors of Greek literature have declined in number, or conceivably see our discipline line up in limbo with classic alchemy.

What expertise society needs and whether political scientists can supply it, the defense continues, are debatable questions and political scientists may well disagree on the answers. But all political scientists ought to be of common conviction that we have arrived at a special body of knowledge which we can lay before others with confidence. How well this body of knowledge suits the current needs of society can hardly be determined until the product is tried out by those who hope to profit from it. A vigorous participation in public affairs is a suitable means for putting our product to test and an open invitation for society to decide whether we are worth what we cost. And delivery of our product in no way impairs our ability to produce more richly in the future. Indeed, the participation by which expertise is made available enriches further scholarship.

The past several paragraphs, offering an imagined indictment and an imagined response, were developed mainly in terms of participation in public affairs with little reference to the special cases of training for public service and administration of educational and improvement programs in foreign countries. The opposing contentions which are set forth apply fully to those special cases.

I have no intention of stating my own position in the debate, since my generous offerings of advice in the past seem not to have accomplished any notable changes in the behavior of political scientists. I may add that I am not certain what are the final points of division among those who join the debate. I suppose all who say that "excessive" participation diverts from scholarship would acknowledge that "a proper amount" of participation enriches scholarship. I suppose all who say that scholarship is greatly enriched by participation would acknowledge that participation can be carried to the point where scholarship loses more than it gains. I suppose also that there will be no general peace of mind on this matter until we turn a little research onto ourselves, finding out just what members of the profession are actually doing, how they distribute their time and effort among their different activities, and what they think they have gained and lost as a consequence of pursuing the many courses they pursue.

part II

THE SCHOLARLY ENTERPRISE

CHAPTER II

What Political Scientists Study

WHAT MAKES A DISCIPLINE?

There appear to be three main points of difference among learned disciplines, three grounds on which they differentiate themselves. These are (1) object of attention or subject matter; (2) kind of knowledge sought about a given subject matter; (3) methods depended upon for getting desired knowledge. Acknowledging the risk involved in oversimplification, we may note some illustrations.

Botany and zoology seem to be differentiated almost solely by the first consideration. One group of scholars fixes its attention on plant life, the other on animal life. The two disciplines, in the main, seek identical kinds of knowledge (e.g., How do cells form and grow? How are characteristics passed on through generations?). Methods depended on for obtaining knowledge have long been near-identical in the two disciplines. Experiments which are executed in the botany laboratory can be duplicated in the zoology laboratory with only a change of the materials brought under examination. The fact that one organism has self-locomotion and the other does not, or that juices are differently propelled through the two organisms, appears to entail only minor adaptations in method of inquiry.

The basic distinction between chemistry and physics appears to lie in the kinds of knowledge which are sought. Chemists and physicists are both concerned with matter, whether animate or inanimate and whether fluid or solid; they ask different kinds of questions about matter. My dictionary states that chemistry investigates the elementary forms of matter and the composition of substances. Physics, says the same dictionary, deals with the states and properties of matter and energy other than those restricted to living matter and to chemical processes. Physicists may be as much concerned as chemists to determine the elementary forms of matter, but physicists do not try to match chemists in the study of how elements combine to form compounds and how elements and compounds are brought together to form mixtures. The great variance of the two disciplines in kinds of knowledge sought entails also notable differences in procedures followed for getting knowledge. It may be that adeptness in particular procedures of inquiry has some effect on what members of the two disciplines decide to inquire into; in the main, however, it must be said that ways of getting knowledge have been adapted to objectives of inquiry and not the other way around.

I am not able to cite two great disciplines whose main ground of variance appears to be in method of pursuing knowledge. But we do have a case of two scholarly groups, each a segment of a discipline—psychologists who study learning and those persons in philosophy departments whom we call epistemologists. Both groups of scholars are concerned to learn something about the human being, and what they want to know about the human being is, on main points, identical. Each wants to know how man arrives at his state of mind; how man acquires his suppositions, his beliefs, his knowledge. It is in method of inquiry that the two groups differ distinctly. Both seek evidence of what exists and occurs in the world external to the scholar, both make inferences from what is observed, both utilize reasoning to relate items of evidence together in elaborate structures. But the two groups of scholars differ in placement of emphasis among these procedures. The psychologist shows great ingenuity in designing his search for evidence; the epistemologist is likely to rely on evidence that comes readily to hand. The epistemologist builds great edifices of reasoning which rest on an insecure evidential base, extending inference and letting guesswork substitute for firm evidence where firm evidence is not easy to come by; the psychologist, in contrast, is conservative in making inferences and allows want of firm evidence to sharply limit the structure he builds by speculation.

The place of political science in the world of organized scholarship can be determined by application of the three tests offered above as differentiating groups of scholars. How does political science relate to other learned disciplines as respects objects of inquiry or subject matter? as respects kinds of knowledge we want or types of questions we ask? as respects methods pursued in getting the kind of knowledge we want about the matters we hold forth to explore? The same three tests are keys to long-standing unhappiness about scholarly effort in political science and current debate about what we can do and ought to do to improve our scholarly product. Have we chosen wisely in identifying a subject matter to be examined? Do we ask the right questions about the subject matter we examine? Is our methodology adequate for getting the knowledge we go after?

It will generally be agreed that the thing which distinguishes American political scientists from other social study disciplines is commitment to a subject matter field, to study of a particular area of affairs, to a terrain. I shall later identify this subject matter or terrain as government of the state (or legal government). This is the one thing which, far more than any other one thing or number of things, gives American political scientists that measure of common character which enables them to be identified as a discipline. As I shall point out later, we appear determined to acquire a full understanding of the government of the state, to stretch our literature out so that it embraces nearly everything man considers worthy of knowing about the governments he has endowed with force for his own regulation. We acknowledge that some aspects of legal government may be passed up by political scientists with expectation that students of law will take care of them. We leave some other matters for attention by the historians or by another social study discipline. But also one hears occasional emphatic assertion that government and politics is a terrain staked out by the political scientists; that for that reason sociologists ought not be writing articles on voting in legislative assemblies and social psychologists ought not be trying to find out how decisions are made in administrative offices of the government.

American political scientists are distinguished by common attention to a particular subject matter. They are not tied together by a common position on either of the other two tests noted above. American political scientists differ greatly in the kinds of knowledge they seek about legal governments and differ greatly in the methods which govern their inquiries. We shall see later that some political scientists wish to contribute to a science of human behavior and seek to apply the methods of inquiry so highly developed by the natural sciences; that another sector of the profession wishes to explore value holdings and ideological commitments and adopts a highly speculative method as main dependence for inquiry; that still another sector (no doubt by far the most numerous) is mainly concerned with the description of institutions, arrangements, and practices and pursues procedures of inquiry which satisfy neither the careful scientist nor the careful student of values.

The differences in the kinds of knowledge we seek and the methods of inquiry we pursue account for the statement so often made that in spite of a common terrain for exploration, American political scientists constitute not one discipline but several disciplines. Some of us, it is said, are (or attempt to be) scientists; some are (or attempt to be) philosophers; some are historians and some are lawyers; and some, who appear not to meet minimum tests for admission to one of the foregoing categories, are only casual reporters of what can readily be observed or are too eager purveyors of action programs that have not been tested by critical scholarship.

The purpose of the preceding paragraphs is to forewarn the reader of what is to come in the remainder of this essay. The pages which follow report the results of my effort to determine what American political scientists have made their subject matter—the terrain they explore; what kinds of knowledge they try to obtain about that area of affairs; what methods they pursue in going after the knowledge they wish to obtain; what differences of viewpoint, of conviction, of commitment divide political scientists when they join debate as to whether the decisions of the profession (made consciously or unconsciously) concerning these matters are wise and ought to govern our scholarly effort in the future.

THE COMMITMENT: FULL UNDERSTANDING OF LEGAL GOVERNMENTS

The central point of attention in the scholarly effort of American political scientists is the government of the state.

We cannot say that attention has been focused on the whole study of the state. The state, as it is defined in the literature of political science, is a population—a collection of people—and the population has a group life that is manifested in many ways other than in government. Political scientists have not, for instance, undertaken systematic inquiry into the complex of goals which state populations appear determined to achieve collectively (e.g., relating to literacy, skills, and disseminated knowledge; relating to production and distribution of goods and services; relating to adjustment of leisure to productive effort), or into the education–direction-control devices by which collective goals are achieved (e.g., religious doctrines and ritual, shared ethical commitments, shared behavior patterns), or into the whole structure of associations which combines the parts of a state population into one great association (including religious organization, business organization, organization for recreation and sports, etc.). Study carried on by political scientists impinges upon and penetrates some distance into these matters. But most, if not virtually all, of such study has been directed to implications for the government of the state, and those studies not so directed are insufficient in number or importance to support a conclusion that the central point of attention for political scientists has moved away from the government of the state.

Neither can we say that the central point of attention for American political science has been the whole study of government. The people who make up a state are only partially governed by organizations that center in national capitol, state house, city hall, county courthouse. Mores support law and extend regulation beyond law. The family supplies education, legislation, and sanction. Religious organizations, economic organizations, and other types of social organization shape states of mind, fix standards of conduct, establish goals and policies, enforce sanctions, and no doubt in other ways complement the government which enacts and enforces law. Political scientists have given attention to these many types of government, but again the inquiries have been mainly directed to implications for the structure of organizations that speak through law.

The central point of attention in American political science, therefore, is that part of the affairs of the state which centers in government, and that kind or part of government

which speaks through law. This is the commitment to subject matter, the terrain which American political scientists
hold forth to explore. For convenience of expression we shall
hereafter refer to this center of attention or terrain as legal
government.

Identification of the terrain to be explored gives only a
clue to the magnitude of the task which the political scientists have undertaken. We must observe what kinds of exploration they intend to make, what kinds of knowledge they
hope to obtain, before we can assess the size of their undertaking and the demands it makes upon them. If all that
chemists want to know about water anywhere in the world
is its chemical composition when in a pure state, they may
conclude that their task is completed when they have arrived
at the formula H_2O. But if chemists want to know the exact
composition of all fluids recognizable as water anywhere in
the world, they may conclude that a good-sized army of
analysts must work constantly at this task through time without end. But generalizations and exact knowledge about the
composition of water constitute only a part, and probably a
minor part, of the vast body of knowledge encompassed in
a full understanding of water. Full understanding may be
thought to include how the components get combined to
form water and divided to decompose water; where water is
found; the relationships of water to animate and inanimate
objects; the uses man makes of water; and so on and so on.

So it is with the political scientists. If they wish only to
establish some basic generalizations about the forms legal
governments take and about the ways in which legal governments do what they do, their job will undoubtedly be ex-
tremely difficult and require an enormous amount of work.
But they will have enormously more work to do if they wish
both to establish these generalizations and in addition to
maintain a standing description of all the variations that
exist in forms of legal government and ways in which legal

governments carry on their activities. And the task grows almost beyond capacity to measure if political scientists extend their descriptive accounts to include the circumstances of emergence and growth and disappearance of legal governments, the relationships of legal governments to other social organizations, the things legal governments do and their impacts on publics; if they go beyond description to identify beliefs people have had about legal governments, subject these ideas to intensive analysis, and evaluate them in terms of a wide variety of tests that may be applied; if description and analysis are to be supplemented by efforts to extend ideas and construct ideal statements of what man can do in the fabrication and utilization of legal governments.

A scrutiny of what American political scientists have addressed themselves to in their scholarly writing and in the courses they teach forces one to these conclusions: (a) We have committed ourselves to acquisition of a full understanding of legal governments; and (b) our vision of what is encompassed in full understanding is sufficiently comprehensive to require inquiry into all the aspects, relationships, and significances of legal government noted in the preceding paragraph. Our task is enormous in magnitude. It commits us to search for many kinds of knowledge. It forces resort to a variety of methods in our effort to obtain the kinds of knowledge we are determined to obtain.

OBJECTIVES AND METHODS OF INQUIRY

The range of matters to which we give scholarly attention and the reliance we place on different methods of inquiry will be examined under the following heads: (1) description of legal governments; (2) examination of ideas; (3) construction of a science; and (4) normative doctrine and proposals for social action.

This classification does not represent a systematic differentiation of types of inquiry. The four heads under which this discussion proceeds were so formulated because they seem to identify four preoccupations predominating in the literature American political scientists produce. In the first draft of this essay I wrote as follows: "Most of our writings having a restricted objective of inquiry, as distinguished from textbooks having more inclusive purposes, are designed mainly to describe what exists and occurs, or to examine an idea or complex of ideas, or to lay foundations for and extend a scientific literature, or to report personal preference and what the author thinks other people should do." I have since examined the book reviews and notes on books in issues of *The American Political Science Review* since 1946 and articles appearing during that period in the same journal and five other American political science journals. I conclude that my original statement was substantially in error. I conclude that I was correct in my identification of four main preoccupations, but wrong in stating that particular studies are directed mainly to one or another of these preoccupations. The truth seems to be that in most cases (I am tempted to say in nearly all cases) any piece of writing, whether book or article, distributes its emphasis among two or more of these four preoccupations. It seems essential, therefore, to say something further at this point about the relation of these preoccupations to one another.

Description I understand to be a report of what actually exists and occurs. Description is based on evidence; the descriptive account reports what has been observed and what is inferred from what has been observed when not everything thought essential to an adequate account is actually observable. I do not mean to suggest that the one who prepares the account must have made the observations himself; he may, of course rely on observations of others, records of past events, and other secondhand materials.

By *examination of ideas* I refer to writing in which reliance on empirical data (evidence of what exists and occurs) is reduced and contributions of the mind are enlarged. It may well be argued that the description that relies most completely on what was actually observed is nonetheless a presentation of ideas. The description is not an array of things observed; it is a verbal statement designed to call up images of things observed. Being a verbal statement, it is a product of the mind and therefore may be called an array of ideas. No doubt all thinking, if you trace the connections back far enough, is rooted in images of empirical reality, but it must be admitted that the mind can put these images together in uncountable combinations. The word *ideas,* in the discussion of literature that follows, will refer to statements in which use of the mind is elaborated, to statements in which contributions of imagination and reasoning add notably to what may have been brought to the mind by direct sensory impression. By *examination* of ideas I mean treatment of ideas in literature by political scientists, which ranges from simple reporting of the ideas of other people through critical examination of ideas of other people to further extension of ideas and development of ideas by the political scientist who is writing.

Construction of a science is a special case of bringing empirical data and ideas together. The objective of science is to describe what actually exists and occurs, but to describe in such a way that each addition to the total descriptive effort points the way to needed further effort. Scientific method imposes upon the student a concern to find out what actually exists and occurs but, more than that, to seek knowledge about reality which is the foundation for obtaining further knowledge. Knowledge that has broadest application is most highly prized. Items of knowledge, arrived at by finding what actually exists or happens under limited observations, are fitted together in statements as to what more generally exists and occurs. These generalized statements (generalizations) which extend to matters not yet investigated are products of the mind, feats of imagination, ideas. They are, for any scientist, hypotheses (grand or limited) until he is of the opinion that they are sufficiently supported by investigation. The investigations that support them, weaken them, or overturn them, are further examination of the evidences as to what actually exists or occurs. The body of belief or knowledge that results from this joining of ideas and evidence is a structure of interrelated generalizations. As the structure of generalizations grows in applicability and acceptance it becomes recognized as a science.

The preoccupation I label *normative doctrine and proposals for social action* is another special case of bringing empirical data and ideas together. I put under this head writing that is heavily impressed by the author's personal preference or conviction. I do so because I think the bolder efforts of American political scientists to construct doctrine relating to values and conduct need to be differentiated from their more objective reporting, analysis, and evaluation of doctrine preferred by others, and because I think their efforts to serve as architects of a social structure need to be differentiated from their more objective efforts to determine effective means for achieving particular ends. Much of our literature that is concerned with values and standards of conduct is discussed, therefore, in the section of this essay headed *examination of ideas;* only the writings that feature the author's own recommendations for commitment and conduct are reserved for later treatment as *normative doctrine.* Similarly, much of the literature that instructs social action is discussed under the headings *description* and *construction of a science;* only writings that are notably influenced by the author's personal convictions are reserved for attention under the head *proposals for social action.*

In view of the meanings I have given those terms, it is obvious that the four heads under which I shall array our literature are not mutually exclusive. Each of the other three heads embraces literature that examines ideas. Scientific inquiry is a special case of description. Normative doctrine and recommendations of social action rest on knowledge of what exists and occurs and provide imaginative descriptions of preferred states of affairs. But while the four heads do not sharply differentiate types of inquiry, they do differentiate major preoccupations or major emphases in the purposes or concerns of writers. One can describe something that exists or occurs without intention to contribute to, and with little likelihood of contributing to, a science; without intention to state what one prefers or would like others to believe or do. One can examine ideas without intention to describe what actually exists and occurs, or to contribute to a science, or to state preference, propose standards of conduct, or recommend social action, and so on.

In general, as I noted above, our writings are not so constructed that individual contributions are devoted mainly to a single one of the four preoccupations. Most striking evidence, perhaps, of mixture of purposes is our general inclination to combine description of what exists and occurs with statements of personal position, normative doctrine, and proposals for social action. In some cases the descriptive part of the item is highly objective, statements of what actually exists and occurs being clearly differentiated from statements of personal position, appeals for acceptance of norms, or recommendations for change in institutions and ways of doing things. In other cases description is mixed up with statements of preference and calls for action, and the reader is left in great uncertainty as to the nature of the reality which purports to be the object of description.

Not all our contributions to literature reveal a multipurpose concern on the part of the author, to be sure. Two sectors of literature in which exceptions to the rule of mixed purposes are most notable should be cited. First, many if not most of the writings that are designed to lay foundations for or advance science—to get us ahead toward generalizations—reveal also a great desire to avoid any preoccupation that would limit the effectiveness of the discourse for achieving its main purpose. Writings that fall in this category differ in the emphasis placed on development of ideas to guide scientific inquiry (construction of theory) and reporting of findings that add to the description of what actually exists and occurs. But such writings generally show careful effort to avoid statements of personal position, normative doctrine, or recommendations for social action. Second, we produce a substantial number of items in which the writer restricts his effort to examination of ideas, making no original exploration of the world of experience to which the ideas relate and avoiding promotion of the writer's own value system. I think, however, that items which are so restricted in purpose are unusual in the body of literature that claims to be primarily concerned with ideas. Most writings that purport to examine and develop ideas represent also an effort to aggrandize the preferences or convictions of the writer, provide normative doctrine, or recommend social action.

Acknowledging their inadequacy for a systematic classification of the literature produced by American political scientists, the four heads I have chosen will nevertheless identify main preoccupations in scholarly effort. They provide a workable base for ordering an account of what American political scientists have given attention to and appear committed to attend to in the future. In the pages that follow we shall observe what American political scientists have studied to date and how they have examined what they have studied, and we shall attempt to determine, by inference from what they have done to date, what the profession appears to regard as its whole assignment in the division of labor among scholarly disciplines.

It is not my purpose, therefore, in the analysis which follows, to allocate to classes the literature produced by American political scientists. Neither is it my intention to pass judgment on the quality of particular writings or on the quality of the whole body of literature we have produced. I shall from time to time cite a book or article, but in all cases the purpose will be to make clear by illustration what kind of study I am talking about, and in no case should it be presumed that the item cited appears to me more worthy than many other items that would have served equally well for illustration. Some judgments about the scholarly character of sectors of our literature also appear; some of them are my own judgments and some of them are the judgments of other political scientists who have put their views in print. In all cases these evaluative statements are subordinated to my main objective, reporting what American political scientists do and what they appear committed to do in the future; the evaluative statement is inserted because it seems the best means of indicating whether much, or perhaps how much, of our collective effort is devoted to a particular type of inquiry. If, for instance, one found that all our descriptions of governmental policies are casual reports of recent innovations in policy, he might conclude that American political scientists are not committed to comprehensive and penetrating description of governmental policies.

Finally, the reader of this report should be aware of certain conclusions I have personally arrived at after recent re-examination of what we have been doing, personal convictions that may affect what I have to say in the following pages no matter how hard I try to keep them from prejudicing my account. They are: (1) The scope of the assignment— viewed as subject matter to be explored and as kinds of knowledge to be obtained—which American political scientists have undertaken is so great that we are challenged to consider whether so many and so various matters can be explored and explained with the thoroughness and the precision expected of any group of men recognized as a learned society and credited with a discipline all their own. (2) Disparity in the kinds of knowledge that political scientists seek to obtain entails significant differences in methods of inquiry and these differences in method in turn create obstacles to common understanding of objectives and achievements and impose difficulties in the training of oncoming political scientists. (3) Doubts and disagreements as to whether we have undertaken to study too much and whether our methods of inquiry are appropriate to our objectives of study are responsible for much of the intellectual conflict which prevails among political scientists today. And (4) the intellectual conflict that grows out of these doubts and disagreements seriously impedes our collective efforts to provide the scholarly product rightfully expected of us by the society that maintains us.

CHAPTER III

Description of Legal Governments

It becomes apparent on the most casual inspection of our literature that American political scientists consider the description of legal governments an important part of their scholarly enterprise. Legal governments constitute the terrain we explore, and descriptive accounts of what exists and occurs are a main device for recording the results of our exploration. We may presume that the profession has not provided for any country the full description of its legal government which is regarded as the goal of American political scientists. We have published enough about different countries, however, to make it clear that the range of phenomena considered relevant and significant to full description is extensive.

OBJECTIVES OF DESCRIPTION

1. *Organizational structure is described.* It is probably safe to say—at any rate it frequently has been asserted—that earlier writings of American political scientists dealt almost exclusively with formal organization, the structure established by law and the supplementary structure that stays fixed sufficiently to be regarded as fairly permanent. This

includes, of course, the main features of lawmaking bodies, of the executive-administrative branch, of the courts, and so on. More recently, efforts at description have extended to what is often called, perhaps quite inappropriately, informal organization. Whether they are formal or informal, the structures that have only lately come in for attention are less permanent in duration, often not officially provided for, often hardly recognized by the people who are caught up in them, but in many cases most significant for full understanding of the whole organizational structure which exists to do the work of government.

Most fully attended to is the national government of the United States. Studies of governmental organization in individual American states that go beyond the superficial level have only lately begun to appear. Municipal, county, and other American local governments have been typed for general descriptive remarks, but intimate accounts of organization for particular cities, counties, and other local governments are rare indeed. Writing about the structure of legal governments in foreign countries is, for most countries, of textbook character; but more probing studies have been made for some, the leading European nations being on this list. Description of international organizations seems also to be well advanced beyond the textbook stage.

2. *The processes of decision-making and action are described.* The dividing lines between processes and organizational structure, as those terms are used here, are not easily traced and it may be that much of what anyone calls process is, when looked at another way, organizational structure. We need not be concerned about nicety of distinction at the moment. The point to be made is that political scientists have tried to find out and state what men and women who are a government do and how they do it. Literature directed to this objective is with few exceptions study of the American national government, and very little of what goes on there

has as yet been described. As late as the present decade we could count as frontier inquiries books such as Stephen Bailey's *Congress Makes a Law* (Columbia University, 1949) and Harold Stein's *Public Administration and Policy Development* (Harcourt, Brace, 1952).

3. *Political scientists attempt to describe the politics of control of legal government.* Writings of this character have many different foci of attention. Earlier works stated who could vote; summarized the laws regulating voting, described arrangements for voting, and brought together a great deal of information about voting conduct (especially fraudulent practices); identified the groupings called political parties; described the organizational structure of parties and the conduct of people who carry on party activities; told how men get nominated for office, how campaigns are conducted, what money is spent for and how money is raised; tried to show how candidates and parties are related to issues of public policy; and provided a great deal of information about the correspondence of the conduct of men in public office to promises previously made and to expectations of the people who elected them. Later studies carry the earlier accounts further in the range of matters described and in the depth to which inquiry is taken. The later attention to what is commonly called pressure groups illustrates the extension in range of attention. V. O. Key's *Southern Politics* (Knopf, 1950) and recent studies of who votes and who does not vote and what classes of people tend to take similar positions in voting illustrate the trend toward greater depth in inquiry. By far the greater part of the descriptive studies relating to the politics of control of government examine experience in the United States, but some studies have been made of experience in other countries.

4. *Political scientists have examined policies and acts of legal governments and their impacts on publics.* Writings of this character are usually evaluative and often are heavily

laden with indications of the writer's preferences, but they provide descriptive accounts of what has occurred. To date, such effort has been spotty in what is selected for examination. Foreign policies of the United States and other countries and particular negotiations and acts of international significance constitute a major part of this literature. Certain controversial subjects of domestic policy in the United States, especially agricultural policy, water resources policy, and a number of matters generally entitled government-labor-business have come in for increased attention in recent years. But relatively little effort has been made by American political scientists to describe policies adopted in many other highly important areas of public concern, such as health, education, marriage and divorce, crime, and conduct which lies at the edges of legality. Lately, study of public policy has been extended to British experience, but few studies of consequence have described experience in other countries.

As yet there has not appeared a rationale that seems to guide political scientists in the selection of policies to be described. It seems proper, therefore, to conclude that the commitment of American political scientists is to describe major ventures in public policy and highly significant acts of government, and the impact of these on publics, in all places having legal government, and perhaps in other places where legal government has not appeared.

5. *Political scientists describe what may be called the human environment of legal government.* It seems fair to say that American political scientists do not consider it their job to describe the physical environment of legal governments. Harold and Margaret Sprout appear to stand alone in studious effort to understand and explain the effect of physical environment—geographic location, physiographic features, climate, etc.—on the development of institutions and the demands placed on institutions (see No. 125). It appears also to be a fact that much of our writing shows little concern about the

human environment that provides the setting in which government is placed and determines the nature of politics. But there is sufficient effort of this character to indicate that political scientists consider it within their assignment to describe those aspects of social structure, of public expectations, and of behavior patterns that appear to have immediate relevance and high significance for establishment, conduct, and control of legal government. Recent developments in literature suggest that political scientists may explore these matters more fully for places outside what is generally called European or Western culture, but there is evidence of growing intent to push the study of American government and politics toward a description of the social structure, belief systems, and commitments of the population that condition the matters thought to be the more central concerns of political scientists.

THE PRODUCT

These summary remarks indicate that the range of phenomena embraced in full description of legal government is startling, if not frightening. To date, efforts at description have been directed mainly to government in the United States, government in other leading nation-states, and organizations that manage relations between nation-states. But we have given some attention to government in lesser states and to the near-equivalents of legal government in other places. The selection of topics for study which has marked our scholarly enterprise to date offers some support for the flippant remark of a colleague that American political scientists are committed to extend their descriptive efforts to legal government or its near-equivalents in every spot on the globe including Andorra and Annam, Monaco and Mozambique, Zanzibar and possibly even the *Zollverein* which flourished about a century ago.

The dispersion of our attention over so great a range and

variety of matters inevitably affects the thoroughness of the descriptive literature produced by political scientists. Invited to describe so many things, we scatter our efforts; only rarely does one political scientist carry forward the description which another political scientist started. The thoroughness of our descriptions is limited also for another reason. The descriptive account is subordinated to another purpose; instead of seeking to provide a full or definitive account of what exists and occurs, the author provides just the amount of description he thinks necessary to support another objective which is the dominant purpose in his writing.[1]

The consequence of subordination of description to other purposes is readily observed in our writing about constitutional law and judicial enforcement of constitutional limitations. Our literature on this subject is voluminous. It is frequently said that this part of our literature is, in quality of analysis, the best that American political scientists have produced. The main purpose in this part of our study has not been to describe a set of relationships that endure with sufficient consistency to be called a system. Rather, the main purpose has been to make clear what meanings the judiciary has given to provisions of the United States Constitution, to show what has happened to legislation as a consequence of judicial determinations of constitutionality, and to evaluate critically the premises and beliefs of judges and the reasoning by which they justified their decisions. The cumulative effect of this literature has been to illuminate brilliantly what judges have done to the national Constitution and what they have done to legislation tested against that Constitution. But if we may say that all that goes on in this business of fixing meaning to constitutional language and deciding the constitutionality of public policy is a system, a describable entity, then it must be admitted that collectively our writings

---

[1] Later in this essay (pp. 83–86) I give reasons for doubt that many of our descriptions contribute significantly to a scientific literature.

do not approach a full description of the system. When you try to fit this literature to the five categories of description listed above, you conclude that it does not, either in single items or collective body of literature, provide anywhere near a full description of the matters contemplated under those heads as they can be related to interpretation and enforcement of constitutions.

(1) Our literature does not provide a full account of the organizational structure for deciding constitutional issues. Political scientists have not given us a thorough report of the general structure of federal courts, or of any state court system, or of the nationwide judicial structure which filters out issues and assigns to different courts particular roles in deciding constitutional issues. Further, if we presume there is more than readily meets the eye in the organizational structure which makes any one court what it is, one must conclude that American political scientists have not yet supplied a full descriptive account of any court. And the apparatus surrounding the court—the relationships of counsel to judges, judge-jury relations, bailiffs and other instruments of the judges, etc.—has not been brought under attention for even casual description.

(2) Our literature does not provide full description of the processes of judicial decision and action. We have made many reports about how justices of the United States Supreme Court divide on particular issues and on types of issues, but have paid little attention to the same matter in lower federal courts and state courts. Judicial biographies have sought to find out what entered into the mind of the judge and affected his decision. But we have reported very little about how judges put their minds together in arriving at common decisions, very little on the role of counsel in influencing decisions, very little on any other matter which presumably has an effect on the decision which is finally made.

(3) Viewed as descriptive writing, our literature of constitutional law and the judicial process has made its greatest contribution to our understanding of how government is controlled. One aspect of control, judicial review of legislative decisions on tests of constitutionality, has been described with thoroughness insofar as the United States Supreme Court is concerned. We have made little exploration of the relationships of lower federal courts to constitutionality of legislation. A start has been made on judicial review of legislation under state constitutions, but it seems fair to say that the notable differences between federal and state practices in this matter have scarcely been noted. Courts participate in control of government in many ways other than by declaring statutes unconstitutional. We have made a start at description of the relations between courts and executive-administrative officials. Control of judges in lower courts by judges in higher courts seems to have been passed by. It may be that political scientists have purposely limited their attention to some of these matters on the supposition that lawyers will provide better descriptions than political scientists can supply; if this be the case, it must be admitted that a charting of what political scientists write about and what they pass over gives little clue to what they consider a proper division of labor between the two professions.

(4) The fourth category of descriptive studies cited above is description of policies and acts of legal governments and their impacts on publics. Declarations of the Supreme Court are primary sources for many of our most important public policies. The national Constitution says that no state shall pass any law impairing the obligation of contracts; the Supreme Court, assisted by lower federal and state courts, decides what is and what is not a contract, what constitutes an obligation that may not be impaired, what kind of legal provision has the effect of impairing an obligation, and so on. Benjamin F. Wright gave us a description as well as an

evaluation of this sector of court-made policy in *The Contract Clause of the Constitution* (Harvard University, 1938). David Fellman very lately did the same kind of a job for court-made policy in respect to a number of constitutional guarantees (*The Defendant's Rights*, Rinehart, 1958).

Books like these two are in the mainstream of our literature relating to constitutions and their enforcement. If our scholarship in this general area is worthy of high praise, it is because of distinguished achievement in describing, evaluating, and criticizing public policies which interpret, extend, and modify the language of the United States Constitution.

But note that what we have so worthily illuminated is court-made policy stemming out of the national Constitution. We have not, as a discipline, won any praise for comprehensive, accurate, illuminating accounts of court-made policy which stems out of language in state constitutions. We have not been denied praise because of inferior effort. We have not even accepted the invitation to try for praise. Note also that what we have won praise for is description, evaluation, and criticism of the policies which come out of the courts, not for probing studies of the social consequences of these policies. I think it will be generally acknowledged that we have at best only begun to explore the impact of judge-made policies on the publics affected by them. Political scientists are now investigating the consequences, in state and community action, of the policy fixed by supreme and lower courts on assignment of whites and Negroes to public schools. We have at least speculated about the consequences, for behavior of individuals and groups, of judicial statements about freedom of speech and press, freedom of assembly, freedom of worship. Few of us have been out in the field to find out how behavior changed when the public policy was clarified or changed. At risk of having overlooked an item I will say that American political scientists have not put in print even one illuminating account of the response of statute-makers to judicial pronouncements or of the steps taken by law enforcement officials and other administrative agencies to strip down the whole body of law they apply and enforce to make it comply with a new judicial instruction.

(5) Finally, our writing about constitutional law and the judicial process does not provide thorough descriptions of the human environment that provides the setting for or conditions the process which is the central point of attention in this literature. I believe I am right in saying that we have not yet produced a careful study of American attitudes toward the national Constitution or any state constitution, toward courts as instruments of government, or toward judicial power when expressed in fixing the meaning of constitutional provisions or expressed in any other way. State constitutions have repeatedly been amended and old ones replaced by new documents since judicial determination of constitutionality was instituted. But I believe we do not have even one probing account of response by constitution-makers to judicial action—i.e., not one account of constitution-making in any state that makes clear to what extent restatement of constitutional language has represented accommodation to judicial interpretation and to what extent it has represented overriding of judicial declarations. Neither, I believe, has any American political scientist published a thorough descriptive account of what actually took place on any of the occasions when the United States Supreme Court or any other court came under extraordinary attack because of widespread dislike for its decisions. Imagination identifies a vast range of matters that may be said to constitute the human environment in which constitutions and courts are placed. It may be that we have provided thorough descriptions of some parts of this human environment; if so I am unable to identify them at this time.

The point of the foregoing remarks is not to say that we have not worked diligently at our study of constitutional law and the judicial process or that we have not produced studies of high quality. I have said many times and am still of the opinion that this may be the best job American political scientists have done to date on any substantial sector of their whole assignment. It may be that our total contribution in this area of study would have been less impressive if greater attention to description had lessened our effort at analysis and evaluation. My purpose in the five preceding paragraphs is only to make clear why I am convinced that the cumulative effect of our writing about these matters does not include a full, thorough, definitive account of what actually exists and occurs. Perhaps every item provides some description. Some things, as noted above, may have been thoroughly described. But in the main, writing in this subject-area has had other objectives than to build up by successive accretions a comprehensive, embracing description of whatever may be involved in this aspect or sector of legal government. Highly suggestive of descriptive study as yet undone is Jack W. Peltason, *Federal Courts in the Political Process* (No. 7d).

If the foregoing conclusions about one of the richest parts of our literature be acceptable, the reader may credit me with sufficient grounds for some additional conclusions— that in virtually all subject-areas of our study, description is subordinated to other purposes; that few individual items in our literature can stand as models of descriptive effort; and that successive items have cumulated to provide thorough-going accounts of what exists and occurs for only a few limited spots in the vast terrain we apparently intend to explore.[2]

---

[2] Descriptive studies are further discussed at a later point (pp. 80 ff.) and illustrative items are there cited.

CHAPTER IV

Examination of Ideas

The objectives of scholarly study by American political scientists include examination of ideas relevant to and significant for full understanding of legal government. The sources of ideas no doubt are beyond determination. All of human experience touches off contemplation, meditation, speculation. This brief discussion of what American political scientists have done with ideas is therefore selective and illustrative. We shall identify some of the chief things political scientists have been doing and not doing, making our choices with concern for the apprehensions of some that we do not do all we should.

We shall direct attention at first to what political scientists have done with ideas that come to them primarily from two sources: literature and belief systems. At the close of this chapter we shall note what has lately been done to develop theory capable of guiding exploration designed to find out what actually exists and occurs. Ideas which enter into the latter type of endeavor come from anywhere and everywhere. The more widely experienced, more thoughtfully read, more richly imaginative the workman, the more abundant his contributions to theoretic structure.

Ideas found in great writings regarded as classics have been the subject of special courses continuously since a discipline of political science became identifiable in this country. In more recent years growing attention has been given to the ideas that enter into great configurations of widespread belief and commitment evidenced not only in writings but in oral expressions and other types of behavior. This is especially the case with those great configurations which, highly integrated and supporting programs of action, get labelled as ideologies.

As is the case with our efforts at description, our accomplishments in examination of ideas fall far short of our commitment. We have scrutinized the offerings of a substantial number of men whose major works are honored as classics, and we have brought under examination the writings of a good many lesser contributors to analysis, speculation, and polemics. But competent critics contend that we have ignored many men whose writings are richer in thought and more worthy of study than those of many other men whose books we have especially combed. These said-to-be-neglected writers include men immersed in non-Western cultures who have written directly and indirectly about government, and men in the Western tradition whose contributions to general philosophy, theology, and fictional literature are believed to have great significance for full understanding of legal government.

Similarly, political scientists are criticized for neglect of some great belief and commitment systems. Surely the great configurations of belief and commitment that are labelled Christianity, Buddhism, and Mohammedanism have high significance for legal government and its role in society; certainly they do not figure in courses in political science and in the writings of American political scientists comparably with such current ideologies as communism and democracy.

Ideas, whether found in literature or in ideologies, are

subjected to different styles of treatment by political scientists which, at this point, may be identified as reporting, restatement and translation, classification and placement, and intensive analysis. Again it should be noted that any particular writing by a political scientist may embrace more than one or even all of these types of examination.

REPORTING

The simplest treatment that can be given an idea is merely to repeat it, perhaps summarizing what was said in greater fullness in the original source. Such an account is not likely to win esteem for the man who provides it, but it is a fact that occasionally a forgotten figure is brought to attention in an article that does little more than supply a simple report of his discourse. Paragraphs, if not whole pages, can be found in textbooks which only state in fewer words what the textbook writer considers to be the most important remarks of the man he is calling attention to.

Essentially the same thing may be said about some of the writing relating to ideologies; main items of belief are stated and main developments in the political movement are pointed out. It may be noted that sometimes, if not always, it is a high achievement merely to identify the ideas that combine to form a state of belief or ideology, and that writing which only reports what the component ideas are is of great significance. Granting these things to be true, it seems fair to add that students who go to the trouble of untangling a complex belief system rarely stop at simple reporting of what the inquiry revealed. They usually, if indeed not always, carry the examination of the component ideas to a stage of critical analysis and offer discriminating comment on the way components combine to form the general belief.

Whether the ideas come from literature, ideologies, or other sources, writing which only reports the existence of

ideas may be a necessary preliminary to scholarship; it seems
to require no further attention in this essay.

RESTATEMENT AND TRANSLATION

The political scientist who wishes to carry examination of
ideas one step beyond simple reporting may try his hand at
restatement and translation. Restatement and translation is
probably an appropriate label for much of the content of
textbooks dealing with the great writings. The author does
more than simply report what the great writer said. He restates the great man's thoughts in language that has more
meaning than the original for the present-day reader; he relates the observations of the man long dead to the preoccupations of the reader now living; he makes explicit the
relevance and significance of the great writing to matters of
present-day concern which the great writer could not have
had in mind when he put his thoughts on paper. In restating and translating for an audience not contemplated by
the originator of the discourse, the student of ideas necessarily performs acts of analysis. But recent criticism of the
literature produced by American political scientists commonly referred to as students of political theory suggests that
most of their restatements and translations are not the fruit
of intensive analysis such as is discussed under that head
later in this essay.

It seems a necessary conclusion also that a great deal of
the presentation of ideas in political science textbooks designed for courses carrying titles other than political theory
is at best only restatement and translation, not intensive
analysis. Perhaps the conclusion is sound also for much of
our non-textbook literature. One man makes statements
about effective organization for government of moderate-
sized cities or cities in the toils of a party machine, and the
rest of us rewrite his statements to make them cover metrop-

olises and small towns, cities with closely matched competing parties, and cities with no political party; and we make the restatement without studious examination of either the reasoning that entered into the original proposition or the evidence that determines its application to additional situations. Careful observation of British experience in devising effective means for attaining certain ends has produced thoughtful statements about placement of authority, limitations of authority, organization, processes, and procedures. American political scientists restate these ideas for an audience that is concerned with evaluation and improvement of American government. Often the treatment of the idea is not marked by intensive effort to identify and attach significance to the likenesses and the differences in conditions prevailing in the two countries (traditions, public expectations, bases for toleration, immediate and long-run goals, etc.) which determine whether and to what extent the propositions born out of British experience have applicability to American needs.

Belief systems, including ideologies, also supply ideas which the political scientist may, by restatement and translation, make more meaningful to others. Ideas that spring up throughout a population seem to bear a relation to the scholar much like that of folk dances and folk tunes to the composer. Many of the forms that characterize enduring music are reproductions of popular dance movements, and many of the melodies that delight us today were the tunes of the countryside and market place a few hundred years ago. The composer may incorporate the dance movement and the tune into his composition with little or no adaptation, or he may refine and reshape the original materials into structure, melody, and harmony which reveal qualities the folk never guessed to be inherent in their productions. Essentially the same can be said of the creation of a great part of our literature relating to government and politics. The idea the scholar puts in his book is found in the expressions of the population; he may discover it through his own attentiveness to common talk or he may encounter it only in the expressions of political leaders, journalists, and other participants in past or current polemics. Like one composer he may restate the folk materials with little refinement or adaptation, or like a greater composer he may extract from the crude productions of the folk an item which he first refines and then elaborates into a statement having a value few suspected to be inherent in the original expressions.

Evidence of willingness to let analysis stop at the level of restatement and translation is surely apparent in most of the writing by American political scientists relating to democracy. Our literature is not wholly barren of original contributions to thought about the ideals, belief-systems, and commitments we label democratic, or about the relation of government to the attainment of democratic ideals, or about the alternative means by which government may be made to conform with democratic ideals. But we shall see, in our later discussion of intensive analysis of ideas, that proportionately very little of the writing about democracy by American political scientists carries analysis beyond the point to which it is taken in literature produced by other people.

CLASSIFICATION AND PLACEMENT

An important objective in the scholarly enterprise of American political scientists is the classification of ideas, the relating of ideas to one another, and the placement of ideas in more inclusive contexts. We do this with ideas found in a wide range of sources, but the character of our efforts can be sufficiently illustrated in our treatment of ideas found in the writings we regard as classics. In addition to reporting what a great man said and translating his discourse for new audiences, we classify his ideas and fix their place in relation to other things. The other things to which we relate one man's idea include (a) his ideas on other matters, (b) the environment in which he wrote and about which he wrote, and (c) the ideas of other men who preceded him or were contemporary with him or succeeded him.

After examining some bibliographies, reading a few brief surveys of writings about classic political literature, and consulting some of my colleagues, I conclude that American political scientists have made very few attempts to bring into one account the most important thought of a great writer on politics. Political scientists in this country apparently have shown little concern to relate to one another a great writer's ideas on different things, seeking to find, for instance, whether his whole body of thought added up to a consistent view of the nature of the state or whether his ideas expressed at different times and directed to different points of interest combined to produce a systematic theory of political relationships. The bibliographies in Professor George Sabine's *A History of Political Theory* (rev. ed.; Holt, 1951) list at least 66 books which, I judge from the titles, purport to examine the whole of a man's political thought; Hans Kelsen's *Die Staatslehre des Dante Alighieri* and Leo Strauss' *The Political Philosophy of Hobbes, its Basis and its Genesis* illustrate. None of the 66 books is by a man I recognize to be an American political scientist except the above two and one by W. Hardy Wickwar, all three of which books were written before the author established residence in the United States. Dealing with the wrong men or appearing too late to get into Professor Sabine's lists are George A. Lipsky, *John Quincy Adams, His Theory and Ideas* (Crowell, 1950); Charles M. Wiltse, *John C. Calhoun* (3 vols.; Bobbs-Merrill, 1944–51); August O. Spain, *The Political Theory of John C. Calhoun* (Bookman Associates, 1951); and Herbert A. Deane, *The Political Ideas of Harold J. Laski* (Columbia University, 1955).

It may be that we are due for a marked increase in publications which examine the whole systems of leading political thinkers. Completed doctoral dissertations listed in the
American Political Science Review during the seven-year
period 1951 to 1957 include 38 which seem to be of this
character. Fifteen of the dissertations deal with Americans,
and few of the men studied are commonly thought of as
great contributors to the literature of politics. The remaining
23 dissertations deal with non-American figures ranging in
importance from such men as Bodin and Harrington to
John Bright and Daniel Defoe.

Painstaking analysis of the whole political thought of a
major figure is a stupendous undertaking and might well be
the job of a lifetime. One might expect to find a greater
number of publications which probe widely in a man's
writings for his ideas relating to a particular matter. Professor Sabine's lists include only one book of this character
that I can attribute to an American political scientist: Willmoore Kendall's *John Locke and the Doctrine of Majority
Rule* (University of Illinois Press, 1941). The considerable
search I have made indicates that if American political scientists have produced other book-length studies of the thought
of one classic writer on one subject, they are indeed few in
number. Articles having this purpose appear from time to
time; examples are: Howard B. White on Burke's views on
political theory and practice (No. 129), Leo Strauss on
Locke's doctrine of natural rights (No. 126), Sheldon S.
Wollin on Hume's conservatism (No. 62), and Howard Penniman on Paine's ideas of democracy (No. 45). I referred
above to 38 completed doctoral dissertations which appear
to examine the whole of a man's political thought; during
the same period 33 dissertations were completed which
examine the thought of one man on a particular subject.

What seems most to attract American political scientists
who study the classic writings is a historical or quasi-

historical treatment of ideas. Primary attention may be given to the special problems that stimulated a man's ideas and the social context that nourished his thought, or primary attention may be given to the development (i.e., refinements, accretions, rejections) of ideas that took place over time and at the hands of many writers. Perhaps the more thoughtful content of all textbooks designed for "political theory" courses provides both lines of analysis; indeed it may be difficult to find even one book-length report of original research that pursues one of these lines of analysis and ignores the other. Illustrating the dual approach are: Charles H. Mc-Ilwain, *The Growth of Political Thought in the West* (Macmillan, 1932); Charles G. Haines, *Revival of Natural Law Concepts* (Harvard University, 1930); Benjamin E. Lippincott, *The Victorian Critics of Democracy* (University of Minnesota, 1938); and Frederick M. Watkins, *The Political Tradition of the West* (Harvard University, 1948). Also illustrative are the following books which treat political thought in the United States: Charles M. Wiltse, *The Jeffersonian Tradition in American Democracy* (University of North Carolina, 1935); Clinton Rossiter, *Seedtime of the Republic* (Harcourt, Brace, 1953); and Louis Hartz, *The Liberal Tradition in America* (Harcourt, Brace, 1955).

The great amount of attention American political scientists have given to classification and placement of ideas has excited some adverse criticism within the profession (see pp. 61–62 below). A reading of even the most severe criticism suggests that we have done a pretty good job of classification and placement; that we have been pretty successful in spotting the significant ideas in great writings, in showing how the idea came out of the times in which it was formulated, in relating ideas to one another, and in placing each man's thought in a stream of literature. The objections filed by the critic seem to fall under other heads. He thinks that a great preoccupation with reporting, restating and translating, classifying and placing has exacted too high a price in neglect of critical evaluation of ideas and further development of ideas; and he thinks that political scientists might better have left to other disciplines the treatment of ideas that make up a good deal of our writing.

What we have accomplished in critical evaluation of ideas and original contributions to further development of ideas is considered later in this essay. On the point that political scientists might better have left much of the study we have undertaken to other disciplines, presumably to students of history and philosophy, the following may be said. The issue turns, for any man, on his presumptions or convictions concerning the central objectives of political science study. If, for instance, one holds that the center of concern is the construction of a science that describes and explains the real world of politics, he may label as intellectual history much of our writing about ideas and argue that these inquiries might better have been made by other disciplines. If one who takes this position restricts his definition of the real world of politics to choice among values and implementation of values through government, he may conclude that much of our writing about how values have been treated in classic literature is irrelevant to a proper study of politics. In that case he may argue that inquiries which reveal how values get identified for expression, how statements about values get passed on to other people, and how one set of value statements relates to other sets throw no important light on how governments effect choice among values and implement values, and so argue further that inquiry into those matters might better have been made by students of history and philosophy than by political scientists.

Such contentions will be refuted by a third man who incorporates a much wider range of matters in his view of what constitutes the central concerns of political science. Earlier in this essay it was pointed out that the profession seems to have as its goal the attainment of a full, not a restricted, understanding of legal governments. Even the least imaginative political scientist will find in "a full understanding" a great number of points from which to start in deciding what is sufficiently relevant to justify scholarly inquiry. If, in deciding what is relevant and significant for political science, one starts with presumptions of full understanding of legal governments rather than presumptions of restricted areas of knowledge, he is not likely to find inappropriate any of the writing political scientists have done about the ideas expressed in classic political literature.

INTENSIVE ANALYSIS OF IDEAS

My colleagues who teach in the Philosophy Department tell me there is no standard nomenclature for the kinds of writing considered in the next few pages and that I am free to fix my own labels. I hope that "intensive analysis" will be acceptable.

Most strictly defined, analysis is the separation of a whole into its elements or constituent parts. As used in the social sciences, I am sure that analysis goes beyond identification of the parts and includes ascertainment of how the parts are related to one another in constructing the whole. The kinds of writing discussed in the immediately preceding pages are analytical in character. The simplest treatment of ideas, reporting what another man said, involves some measure of analysis because one cannot reduce the fuller statement to summary language without first discerning differentiable parts in the original statement. Efforts to restate and translate are a further advance in analysis, and classification and placement of ideas, when highly thoughtful, penetrating, and exacting, represents a high order of analytic effort. All of the publications cited above as illustrations of classification and placement of ideas serve equally well as illustrations of what I here call intensive analysis.

But the discussion in the next few pages embraces also some kinds of writing that go beyond the identification and ordering of component parts (analysis as defined above). Thus, writing which critically evaluates the ideas presented by other people, and writing which gives fuller development to ideas or extends their application are treated here as intensive analysis. We shall, however, reserve for later treatment writing which is designed primarily to establish and justify the personal preferences and convictions of the writer. I suppose that in virtually all thoughtful writing about ideas the author evaluates propositions against tests of validity selected by him, and that in so doing the author injects his own value premises into the discourse. We shall treat such discourse as intensive analysis so long as it falls short of that bold declaration of personal preference which would throw it into the category to be discussed in the next chapter: Normative Doctrine and Proposals for Social Action.

A comprehensive and systematic treatment of our literature which attempts intensive analysis of ideas would make demands far beyond my ability to satisfy. I shall direct my remarks to three centers of attention, believing that some general commentary on each of them will both establish the fact that American political scientists do provide some analysis of high quality and indicate why many members of our profession think we provide far too little of it. My three heads will be: (1) Study of Classic Literature; (2) Study of Ideologies; and (3) Development of Empirical Theory.

1. Study of Classic Literature

It was noted in previous paragraphs that American political scientists who write about the classics have been adversely criticized on the ground that they place too much emphasis on reporting what the great men said, restating and translating their discourse, placing their writings in the social context that produced them, and relating writers and the ideas they developed to other writers and other ideas. Much of this literature produced by American political scientists can also be adversely criticized on the ground that it does not represent high-quality scholarship. Simple reporting and perhaps much of the effort to restate and translate is deficient on that test. But studies that relate writers to their times and to one another and classify and place ideas challenge the author to diligent search and penetrating analysis, and I think it will be generally agreed that the best of our writing of this character stands up in quality with the best that has been done by political scientists in other countries or by students in other disciplines.

The charge that American political scientists who study the classics have misdirected their efforts, giving undue attention to matters that had better be left to students of history and philosophy, should not be interpreted to mean that the critics think we have done no writing that goes beyond classification and placement. We produce critiques of the propositions and argumentation found in the classics. We extend the analysis provided by the great writer, examining considerations he overlooked or thought unimportant. We test the propositions in the classic by fuller reference to the facts of life which determine whether those propositions are meaningful and fix limits to their significance for an enduring literature. And we branch out from the base which classic literature provides to develop ideas which owe their character much more to the political scientists who developed them than to the men long dead who may have suggested them.

Having acknowledged that American political scientists have produced some literature, based on or stemming out of the classics, which is of highest quality, I am obliged none-theless to report a conclusion that we have not produced a great deal that stands up with the best provided by students in other disciplines or students in other countries. I counted the books (but not the articles) entered in the bibliographies in Sabine's *A History of Political Theory* (rev. ed., 1950). Of 419 entries (books listed more than once were recounted), only 32 were written by men I could identify as American political scientists. And I got 32 by including one transla-tion (with critical introduction) and by counting four entries for Hans Kelsen, Hans Kohn, and Robert M. MacIver who may be thought not to belong in the category of American political scientists. The 32 entries included 26 different books written by 22 American political scientists. It may be that a count which includes only books and excludes articles is unfair to American political scientists, since it may be that differences in writing practice and publication outlets cause us to put in journals what Europeans would put in books. I think this is not an excuse for us, however; a casual examination of the articles listed by Professor Sabine indicates that American political scientists would not show up well on that count either.

Professor Sabine's listings should give us a guide to pub-lications that classify and place the classic writings and evalu-ate and criticize them. Since his book is a history of political theory, we may suppose that he did not put in his bibliog-raphies writings in which a concern to show how far the great men carried an idea is notably subordinated and the author's principal concern is to present his own development of the idea. The kind of writing I have in mind is illustrated by Westel W. Willoughby, *The Fundamental Concepts of Public Law* (Macmillan, 1924) and *The Ethical Basis of Political Authority* (Macmillan, 1930); William Y. Elliott, *The Pragmatic Revolt in Politics* (Macmillan, 1928); J. Roland Pennock, *Liberal Democracy: Its Merits and Pros-*

pects (Rinehart, 1950); and articles by Lowell Field and Max Shepard on jurisprudence (Nos. 21, 84); Charles Nixon and David Spitz on civil liberty (Nos. 117, 56); and the debate on majority rule by Herbert McClosky, Willmoore Kendall, and J. Roland Pennock (Nos. 78, 75, 46).

The few items just cited by no means exhaust the list of books and articles in which American political scientists carry ideas well beyond the point where they found them in literature. A complete listing, I am sure, would reveal that we have been far less productive than any of us would wish. This conclusion finds support in recent commentary by David Easton and Benjamin Lippincott. In his discussion of "the decline of political theory" in *The Political System* (Knopf, 1953), Easton states that American political scientists consider value to be the heart if not the whole of political theory (pp. 233–34) and concludes after some analysis of our writing that American political scientists "have so construed the consequences flowing from their conception of values that they are forestalled from attempting a radical reconstruction of their moral heritage. They are driven to assume that, aside from historical description, their major task in moral matters is to clarify, like extreme semanticists, and not to construct, like imaginative moral architects" (p. 254).

In his contribution to the UNESCO volume (No. 1), Lippincott evaluates the literature of political theory produced in the United States. By political theory, he says, "I mean a systematic analysis of political relations" (p. 208). American writers, he finds, "have given us a great deal of history and relatively little theory" (p. 214). "The paradox is that there has been more creative work done in political theory by men outside the professional field [political science] than by those within it" (p. 220). "Although the very essence of political theory lies in a systematic analysis of political relations, not more than five writers [of the United States] in political sci-

ence have made a serious attempt at such an analysis" (p.
211). The five he lists are Westel W. Willoughby, Charles E.
Merriam, John Dewey, Walter Lippmann, and Robert M.
MacIver. Some political scientists may think our profession
ought not claim all five of these. The titles Lippincott cites
are, in all cases, books; it is possible that he would alter his
statements somewhat if he had more prominently in mind
our contributions in article form. My own limited inspection
of recent volumes of American political science journals
causes me to think that inclusion of articles in his appraisal
would not significantly alter Lippincott's evaluation of the
contributions we have made.

2. Study of Ideologies

If, as I suppose, the commitment of American political
scientists includes thoughtful analysis of ideas found in ideologies which have significance for legal government, it must
be admitted that we have not yet made notable progress in
meeting that part of our obligations. Religions appear to be
virtually untouched. Certainly no American political scientist has provided a noteworthy analysis of the idea-system
(or idea-systems) that characterizes religions in general.
Neither has an American political scientist carefully explored the significance for legal government of the belief-
system, organizations, and rituals we call Christianity. I am
told that most of our writing that deals with Christianity
falls in the class Easton and Lippincott label historicism,
and that the remaining part of this writing is tentative, tan-
gential, or limited in what it undertakes to examine. Our
histories of political theory acknowledge the emergence and
development of Christianity, examine the thought of the
Church Fathers, Thomas Aquinas, Luther, Calvin, and so on.
When we write about the course of political thought in this
country, we give the Puritans their proper place in the account. The occasional appearance of a monograph such as

Frank Grace's *The Concept of Property in Modern Christian Thought* (University of Illinois Press, 1953) adds a dimension of depth to our literature. But, laid side by side, these varied approaches to the subject do not supply a broad or a firm base for evaluating the significance of religion for politics. The intensive analysis of what Christianity, as belief-system or social organization, signifies in our time is left almost wholly to others (Barth, Maritain, Niebuhr). If Christianity has been put on the agenda of American political science, it is for serious attention at a later date. The same thing must be said concerning the other great religions.

The ideas (suppositions, beliefs, convictions) which are essential to democracy and which distinguish it from nondemocratic or antidemocratic ideologies ought in anyone's estimate be especially challenging to the American political scientist. Surely we are deeply concerned to understand and help others understand the ideals that give democracy its essential character, the relation of legal government to democratic ideals, the conditions (commitments, social organization, etc.) requisite for the establishment and maintenance of democratic government, the instrumentalities (institutions, arrangements, ways of doing things) by which government is in fact made democratic.

American political scientists have put in print some illuminating analysis of these matters, but not much of it. Again I checked a bibliography. Roland Pennock listed about 350 titles (books and articles) in his *Liberal Democracy: Its Merits and Prospects* (Rinehart, 1950). Men I recognize as American political scientists account for 61 of the entries. But fully a half of these items seem to be a long way removed from central issues in democratic theory (e.g., Corwin's *The Commerce Power versus States Rights* and Galloway's *Congress at the Crossroads*). I am confident that a reading would reveal that many of the remaining items deal only tangentially with ideas essential to democracy. Still other items would have to go out, I am sure, on the ground that they do not provide intensive analysis as we have been using that term here. When you complete this process of elimination, you end up (assuming that Pennock started us off with a good base list) with a pretty small number of books and articles in which American political scientists have sought to provide careful and thoughtful analysis of ideas essential to democracy. Their contribution is important, but it does not loom up impressively when compared with the writings of men in other countries and other disciplines.

I have not made a similar check into the literature dealing with fascism and communism. I am told by students of the subject that American political scientists have provided some thoughtful analysis of the ideas basic to those ideologies, but that their contribution is minor when compared with the scholarly writing emanating from British and other European authors and Americans who cannot be claimed as political scientists. Some American political scientists are at the front in empirical study of great political movements and it may be they are leaders in analysis that develops guides for further research. We deal with the latter type of effort in the next several paragraphs.

3. Development of Empirical Theory

This title may inadequately characterize a new turn in our literature. A number of political scientists, almost none of whom had appeared in print before World War II, have contributed analysis which promises to redirect the course of scholarship in this country. It would be gross error to say there are no worthy models of this kind of effort in prewar literature. At the least it must be admitted that the tempo of production has increased remarkably since the war; I think it fair to say that there has lately been an unprecedented release of imagination in the search for what is relevant and significant for a wide range of objectives in study.

Acknowledging again that I may be an incompetent reporter, I suggest that the young people who have given this new turn to our literature have these goals in mind. (1) They seek to refine the concepts which fix points of inquiry and control the results of inquiry, and seek to establish precise labels which enable these concepts to move from student to student with minimum chance for misunderstanding. (2) They hope to construct theory—ordered arrays of propositions—which discipline the mind in identifying, evaluating, and interpreting evidence. And (3) they propose and try out—in some cases diligently execute—research designs which give promise of turning up the facts which theory declares essential to sure understanding of what exists and occurs.

Intensive analysis of this character is surely indispensable to probing, revealing description of the real world. Its value extends far beyond the descriptive endeavor, however. Refinements in conceptualization and precise statements about how significant matters are related to one another provide a platform from which some students take off on the most scientific pursuits and others set out on the most speculative or philosophical inquiry. If some members of our profession put a low value on this new current in our literature it must be that they think achievement to date has not been worthy of the ambition which stimulates these young scholars.

There is general recognition that communication among political scientists is seriously hindered by inadequate concepts and by failure to reach agreement on labels to be attached to concepts that have been elaborated and found useful. Use of the word "authority" in literature relating to public administration will illustrate. Author A writes, "The director wished to terminate this procedure but did not have sufficient authority to do so." And A does not in his further discourse make clear what meaning he gives to the word "authority." Reader R cannot tell whether A meant to say: (1) that statutes or other expressions of law did not make clear that the director could do what had to be done in order to terminate the procedure; or (2) that the director was inhibited by factors in his environment from attempting to do something the statutes appeared to make available to him as a course of action; or (3) the director did do something but people to whom he addressed himself did not respond in accordance with his wishes; or (4) something else. If A was clear in his own mind as to what he meant, the breakdown in his communication to R could be charged to lack of agreement on labels to be attached to highly developed concepts. If, on the other hand, A hadn't realized that the difference between what happened and what the director wished would happen could be due to any of the three (and possibly additional) considerations just mentioned—in that case both analysis and communication suffered from inadequate development of concepts. An examination of the literature relating to public administration makes it clear that the word "authority" has not been nailed to one and only one meaning or image of relationships, supports a conclusion that many political scientists have used the word "authority" without being clear in their own minds as to what meaning or image they wished to convey to the reader, and invites a suspicion that some political scientists have examined situations without adequate awareness that many different conditions may account for the failure of a man to make his wishes effective.

Conscious effort to formulate, refine, and clarify concepts and to obtain agreement on labels to be attached to concepts does not always meet with universal approval. Disapproval is likely to be expressed in two words of opprobrium— "hairsplitting" and "jargon."

When the critic charges me with hairsplitting I understand he means to say that I have made distinctions or differentiations that are not meaningful, not significant, or not economic for analysis or communication. I suppose that some efforts at formulation of concepts are properly subject to this charge. The distinctions and differentiations may be too fine for usefulness. They may represent extensions of logic which identify situations that do not correspond with any situations we have yet discovered or believe may be discovered in the real world, or which, if thought to exist in the real world, are of such a character that we cannot apply to them the niceties of distinction and differentiation proposed by the formulation. Many charges of hairsplitting, however, are arguable. Scholarship advances at frontiers of understanding. One man sees hope of progress in analysis which another man feels confident is a blind alley. One man thinks that, to push inquiry ahead significantly, we need to make distinctions and differentiations which another man thinks we are not ready for and, because they are premature, will result in confusion and retard meaningful inquiry rather than advance it. Finally, it should be said that many charges of hairsplitting undoubtedly reflect sloppy thinking or laziness on the part of the man who makes the charge. He just isn't up near the frontiers of contemporary analysis, or he is unwilling to take the next steps his judgment tells him have to be taken.

The charge that some of us express ourselves in jargon is often a way of saying that we do what I cited above as hairsplitting, but it more specifically expresses objection to the labels attached to the concepts we formulate and develop. No doubt some of the labels are found offensive for good cause. Men who are dominated by concern to get ahead sometimes like to show off. Some of them wish to be known as father of a phrase. They like to be thought learned, or ingenious, or maybe just different from others. So they may select a word or concoct a word or invent a word that is more effective for startling the reader than fixing in the reader's mind a connection between the word as label and the set of ideas which the label is attached to.

It is equally certain that much of the objection to new terms which comes out under the charge of jargon is simple unwillingness to face the need for quick and easy ways of identifying a precise and firm set of ideas which promise usefulness in pushing inquiry ahead and reporting to other people the results of inquiry. It may be that some political scientists need to ponder the experience of the medical profession. I tell my doctor that I have broken my leg below the knee, but when he writes his report the phrase "broken leg" does not appear in it. I have a fracture of either the tibia or the fibula or both, and the fracture is either simple, or compound, or simple comminuted, or compound comminuted. I do not understand that the doctors use these terms simply to delude or impress their patients. These technical words identify differentiable objects in the body and differentiable conditions within those objects or affecting them. Precise images are called up in the mind of one doctor when another doctor uses these words. If the development of concepts by members of the group (physicians or political scientists) is dominant and the fixing of labels to identify the concepts is secondary (labels are adjusted to concepts rather than the other way around) analysis goes forward and communication is effective.

Development of concepts is a collaborative enterprise, and the enterprise is carried on in various kinds of writing. The student who plans a research undertaking finds it necessary, in order to point up his study and manage data, to structure the world of affairs he intends to examine in a manner different from the way it has been structured in previous literature; i.e., he makes identifications and differentiations that vary from the identifications and differentiations other students and lay observers have made. When research is completed, recommendations are made for revision of the concepts used in the study and for development of additional concepts. The early studies of "pressure groups" by Childs, Herring, and Odegard, and the later refinements and additions to their identifications and differentiations by Truman and others illustrate formation and restatement of concepts in connection with empirical inquiry. The critic of the research enterprise, in book review or in synthesis of research to date, points out inadequacies in concepts and proposes revisions and substitutes, e.g., Dwight Waldo, *The Administrative State* (Ronald, 1948) and Lawrence Herson's critique of the textbooks in municipal government (No. 26). The process goes on in writings of the kind we have already discussed under the heading of intensive analysis of ideas. Finally, textbooks contribute to development of concepts. The concepts relied upon in the study of public administration in this country were largely developed in textbooks, the main contributors including Leonard D. White, *Public Administration* (Macmillan, 1926); William F. Willoughby, *Principles of Public Administration* (Brookings Institution, 1927); and Herbert A. Simon, Donald W. Smithburg, and Victor A. Thompson, *Public Administration* (Knopf, 1950). Illustrating the role of textbooks in clarifying concepts useful in other areas of study are: Bertram Gross, *The Legislative Struggle* (McGraw-Hill, 1953); Ernst B. Haas and Allen S. Whiting, *Dynamics of International Relations* (McGraw-Hill, 1956); and Avery Leiserson, *Parties and Politics* (Knopf, 1958).

Literature of the types just mentioned appears not to have satisfied our needs for concepts to guide further inquiry. In any event, during recent years, and especially since World War II, American political scientists have taken a new look at their concepts and labels and have made a head-on effort to straighten them out in several areas of study. In some instances this effort takes the form of an article concerned only with the problem of concepts and labels. In other cases it comes as an article or book which goes beyond concepts and labels to develop theory that will guide further study. In a few cases we are given a volume which tries to go the whole distance; it restates basic and subsidiary concepts and labels them, sets forth theoretic propositions to guide research, describes a research design, and then reports the findings arrived at by carrying out the research plan. At risk of offense because of failure to mention some areas where fruitful work is going on, I will note three focal points of imaginative effort in current development of concepts, theory, and research design.

First, definite progress is being made in clarifying concepts significant for study of administration. Effort which political scientists have devoted to this cause was stimulated mainly, no doubt, by Chester I. Barnard's *Functions of the Executive* (Harvard University, 1938) and the several studies by Elton Mayo and his associates. Definite progress has also been made since the war in formulating theory and elaborating research design but I think political scientists must admit this has been mainly a gift of the sociologists (Selznick, Blau, Gouldner typify). Without further differentiation of points of emphasis—concept, theory, design—we may note some main contributors in the ranks of political science. Herbert A. Simon's *Administrative Behavior* (Macmillan, 1947) stands at the head of a current in our literature. Simon's influence was extended in the textbook, *Public Administration* (Knopf, 1950) which he wrote in collaboration with Donald Smithburg and Victor Thompson and in a number of articles (see in the list of references Nos. 54, 85, 99 and No. 4 at p. 23). Robert A. Dahl and Dwight Waldo have also been highly influential. For Dahl's offering see Dahl and Lindblom, *Politics, Economics, and Welfare* (Harper, 1953) and in the list of references No. 4 at p. 45, and No. 90. Waldo's first significant analysis appeared in his *The Administrative State*

(Ronald, 1948). His more notable contributions in the journals are Nos. 61 and 127. Edwin O. Stene lent his hand to the cause in a pamphlet-sized analysis, *American Administrative Theory* (University of Kansas, 1950). Fritz Morstein Marx very recently contributed his *The Administrative State: An Introduction to Bureaucracy* (University of Chicago, 1957). Other significant contributors who first came to attention since World War II are Arch Dotson (No. 106), Murray Edelman (No. 91), James Feeley (No. 20), Morton Grodzins (No. 92), Herbert Kaufman (No. 29), Verne Lewis (No. 94), Norton Long (Nos. 95 and 96), Arthur Maas and Lawrence Radway (No. 97), Phillip Monypenny (No. 116), Fred Riggs (No. 6 at p. 23), Glendon Schubert (No. 52), Donald Smithburg (No. 86), and Frank Sorauf (No. 87). Dwight Waldo reviews this current in our literature relating to public administration, noting contributions from both within and without the political science profession, in *The Study of Public Administration* (No. 7b). See also the essay by William Siffin in No. 6 at p. 1.

Second, truly remarkable strides have been taken in study of international affairs since World War II. Concepts relating to international law have long been highly developed because those who formulate, enunciate, and interpret rules of law are highly conscious of the need to make precise identifications, differentiations, and definitions. Statesmen and diplomats have not impressed a comparable preciseness on the language of international politics. Neither have students of international politics, in spite of the great amount of writing throughout centuries, brought a satisfactory order into their search and analysis. In any event, like students of administration, they have made a head-on effort since World War II to revise and clarify concepts useful in their area of study, to construct theoretic propositions which provide imagined descriptions of the terrain to be explored, and to design research which will replace theory with sure knowledge. The most impressive effort of this character by a single scholar, no doubt, is that by Quincy Wright in his *The Study of International Relations* (Appleton-Century-Crofts, 1955). Much of the analysis which, viewed against traditional ideas and terms, appears most inventive and innovative has been supported by foundation grants and in most cases represents collaborative effort. Among the more important items so characterized are: Richard C. Snyder (No. 7 at p. 3) and Snyder with H. W. Bruck and Burton Sapin, *Decision-making as an Approach to the Study of International Politics* (mimeographed, Princeton University, 1954); the "elites and symbols" studies by Harold D. Lasswell, Daniel Lerner, Ithiel de Sola Pool, and others, carrying the common title *Revolution and the Development of International Relations* ("Hoover Institute Studies," Stanford University, 1951 and later); and several items by Karl W. Deutsch and his associates including *Nationalism and Social Communication* (Wiley, 1953), *Political Communication at the International Level, Problems of Definition and Measurement* (No. 7a), and *Political Community and the North Atlantic Area* (Princeton University, 1957). Two other bold ventures are Morton A. Kaplan, *System and Process in International Politics* (Wiley, 1957), and George Liska, *International Equilibrium: A Theoretical Essay on the Politics and Organization of Security* (Harvard University, 1957). Less startling to students in an earlier tradition but nonetheless conscious of need for clarification of concepts are Gerhart Niemeyer, *Law Without Force, The Function of Politics in International Law* (Princeton University, 1951); and Percy E. Corbett, *Law and Society in the Relations of States* (Harcourt, Brace, 1951). Articles designed to put the study of international politics on a sounder basis include contributions by Maurice Ash (No. 101), Ernst B. Haas (Nos. 24, 73, 108), Robert L. Humphrey (No. 74), Morton Kaplan (No. 109), Charles McClelland (No. 113), Harold and Margaret Sprout (No. 125),

and Kenneth W. Thompson (No. 59). It should be noted that
political scientists are greatly aided in this part of their enterprise by students in other disciplines, prime contributors in
this country including Feliks Gross, Harold Guetzkow, F. S. C.
Northrup, and Donald Taft.

Third, we are making a new effort to straighten out our
thinking about democratic government. Two small books
which appeared since World War II put theory of democratic government on a new level: Robert A. Dahl, *A Preface
to Democratic Theory* (University of Chicago, 1956), and
Anthony Downs, *An Economic Theory of Democracy* (Harper, 1957). Dahl's book is distinguished by rigor of analysis.
It is imaginative and stubborn in critique of concepts and
propositions found in other writings. It lays foundations for
new ventures in theory of democratic government, both descriptive and normative. Downs contributes a daring and
courageous effort to construct a theory of how major issues of
policy might be decided by a government that acted rationally
to maximize popular approval. J. Roland Pennock's *Liberal
Democracy: Its Merits and Prospects* (Rinehart, 1950), mentioned above, is relevant here. The textbook by Ranney and
Kendall designed for courses in political parties (*Democracy
and the American Party System,* Harcourt, Brace, 1956) takes
great care to establish meaning for the word democracy and
other related terms. Felix Oppenheim has pressed for language of high precision in several articles (Nos. 44, 81, 118).
Three articles by Herbert McClosky, Willmoore Kendall, and
J. Roland Pennock deal more specifically with the concept of
majority rule (Nos. 78, 75, 46). See also Neal Riemer (No. 122).
In my own opinion, study of instruments of democratic government is greatly handicapped at present by failure to clarify
our concepts and avoid the resultant confusion in our literature relating to political parties, representative assemblies, correspondence of official action and public expectations, and
kindred matters. Robert Dahl in *Congress and Foreign Pol-*

icy (Harcourt, Brace, 1950), Alfred de Grazia in *Public and Republic* (Knopf, 1951), David Truman in *The Governmental Process* (Knopf, 1951), Bertram Gross in *The Legislative Struggle* (McGraw-Hill, 1953), and Roland Young in *The American Congress* (Harper, 1958) try to replace confusion with order in important areas of this great field of study. Recent efforts to firm up concepts and fix definitions and terms relating to what is commonly called voting behavior are reviewed and evaluated in *Handbook of Social Psychology*, edited by Gardner Lindzey, vol. 2, chapter 30 (Addison-Wesley, 1954), and by Peter Rossi in *American Voting Behavior*, eds. Eugene Burdick and Arthur J. Brodbeck (The Free Press, 1959), pp. 5–54. For further review of these efforts see articles by Samuel Eldersveld (No. 70) and Warren Miller (No. 115), an essay by Alfred de Grazia (No. 4 at p. 104), and a booklet by Neil A. McDonald, *The Study of Political Parties* (No. 7e).

CHAPTER V

Construction of a Science

The commitment of American political scientists includes the development of a literature that is scientific in character. We are one of several disciplines that prefer to be known as social sciences rather than as social studies. We have for several decades officially designated our particular discipline as political science and those of us who find the word science inappropriate because a misnomer or too restrictive appear to be definitely a minority of the profession.

WHAT IS BEING SCIENTIFIC?

In Chapter IX of this essay we discuss intellectual conflict within the profession relating to the scientific character of our scholarly enterprise. The conflict that plagues us on this score centers on the emphasis to be placed on scientific inquiry, proper subjects of scientific inquiry, and how best to undertake scientific inquiry. It appears doubtful that any American political scientist would contend that there is no place whatever for application of scientific method in the study of legal governments. No doubt every political scientist will acknowledge that some things we need to know about legal governments are best found out by study that tries to meet accepted tests of scientific inquiry.

The meanings given to the terms science, scientific inquiry, scientific method are not constant among different disciplines and among persons within a particular discipline. Here they will be given liberal rather than restrictive meanings. In this essay we shall say that a political scientist pursues scientific study (1) if he has as his object of inquiry a matter that can be illuminated by empirical evidence, (2) if he accords to empirical evidence highest probative force, (3) if in search for, analysis, and evaluation of evidence he approaches the highest standards other social scientists have proved to be attainable, and (4) if he reports his procedures and his findings in a way that affords other students ample opportunity to judge whether his evidence supports his findings. Studies carried out in this way will be called scientific inquiries. And scientific inquiries providing findings that can be fitted, immediately or later, into generalized statements about relationships that exist and persist will be viewed as contributing to a structure of belief and knowledge entitled to be called science.

The foregoing statements will not satisfy students in the natural sciences, say astronomy or physics. They demand that conclusions rest on evidence that can be verified by the observations of other students. The object of natural science inquiry does not speak to one man and thereafter remain silent; it does not evidence its character this way today and thereafter give essentially different evidences of its character. If student B carefully reproduces the accurately described experiment of student A, then B should find essentially the same things that A reported. This is not to say that a given planet always will be found at the predicted spot in relation to other planets, or that a gaseous element called helium will always appear to behave the same way to different observers. But the natural scientist assumes that when careful observations reveal significant discrepancies, the discrepancies are due to conditions not yet accounted for, and that when those conditions are identified and taken into account, further careful observations will turn out to be essentially in accord. If all that affects the behavior of helium is pressure and temperature, then when pressure and temperature are identical in a series of observations, helium should evidence near-identical behavior to all careful observers. Because their observations to date do reveal a high uniformity in the evidences of what exists and what occurs in nature, the natural scientists are able to formulate generalized statements of what can be expected to happen in the future when certain things come together in certain ways under specified circumstances. These generalizations constitute the most enduring part of the literature they call their science.[1]

If, in the study of human relationships, we restrict the term scientific method to pursuit of evidence available in near-identical form to all observers, we deny that label to much of our most careful evidence-seeking inquiry. Student A carefully records everything (presume that it is possible to do so) that goes on among a group of men discussing a problem—what they say (including intonations and gestures) and what they do. His findings can never be verified with the exactitude possible for students of natural phenomena. The same men will never meet again to discuss the same problem under the same circumstances. The sum of our experiences, including what was observed in A's study, tells us that what happens in a meeting is greatly affected by many things we cannot know including what each member of the group sees at stake in the decision, the intensity of his convictions, his emotional state, and the previous relations of the members to one another. You do not repeat another man's observa-

---

[1] I am aware of the risk incurred in making either casual or studied statements about what scientists do and what science is. How to think and speak about these things is a major concern of the highly controversial literature called "philosophy of science."

tions and verify or disprove his findings when you admit that the matter he observed contained factors of high relevance and significance not known to be present in the matter you observe. If we are not able to identify, take into account, and allow for all factors that figure significantly in the matter we observe, we have no sure base for generalizations. Even if a dozen careful students observing a dozen meetings report a common occurrence—one man calls another man a liar and thereafter neither says a word—we are unwilling to make a generalization that always, or even ordinarily, when men meet to discuss a problem one will call another a liar, or that if one does call another a liar both will thereafter remain silent.

No doubt some generalizations about behavior of human groups can be supported by observations repeatable with sufficient exactitude to give them scientific status among the most demanding of the natural scientists. Granting this, we still must acknowledge that many, and no doubt most, findings about human groups which social scientists count highly significant cannot be subjected to that degree of verification. One must conclude that, if the definition of scientific method is fixed by the natural scientists, very little of the study of human relationships can be carried on in strict compliance with scientific method. I do not understand that they have been given a monopoly on definition of the term. I think that students of human relations are entitled to call their efforts scientific when they approach as closely as they know how to the model set for them by students who deal with natural phenomena. Being of that mind, I suggest that the political scientist is pursuing scientific method if he makes a conscientious, careful, systematic effort to find out what actually exists and goes on, and reports his findings in a way that enables other students to evaluate the sufficiency of his evidence for his conclusions and to test his findings by further studies as nearly identical to his own as may be possible. Study carried on by pursuit of such method is therefore scientific inquiry.

I am not willing to say, however, that the cumulation of a number of scientific studies makes a science. It seems to me we should not claim to have produced a literature entitled to be called a science of politics unless we are convinced that we have formulated a substantial body of generalizations that fit together in a structure of knowledge (warranted belief). A scientific inquiry into the relationships among men forming a group produces trusted findings as to what occurred in the group which was studied; these findings become part of a science only when they are fitted with other findings to support trusted generalized statements about relationships of men in typified groups.

I say trusted generalizations rather than proven generalizations. It is sometimes said that students of natural phenomena can create a science because there is a uniformity in nature which assures them that once they have found out how nature behaves under certain identifiable circumstances they can tell you how nature will always behave under those circumstances. This presumes too much. All the natural scientist knows (barring divine revelation) is how nature behaved when observed. When he says what will happen in the future, he assumes a risk. As identical observations increase, he is entitled to increased confidence in his generalizations and the risk in making them is reduced. But what will happen in the future is not proven until it happens. The history of any natural science reveals a great number of generalizations thought to be dependable by men of highest scientific repute in one generation but rejected as error by a later generation. It is to be expected that many generalizations which present-day students of natural science think firmly established will be upset by further study.

Scientific inquiry is assisted by many kinds of writing that are not scientific in character. Closely associated with the scientific study are the previous efforts at clarification of concepts and development of theory (discussed at pp. 64–74 of this essay) which help the student decide what he wants to look for and guide him in designing the specific inquiries he will pursue by scientific method. Previous descriptions and even rank speculations about the matters he intends to investigate help the student to anticipate the character of the data he will encounter in his scientific pursuit, and provide presumptions about reality against which he may check his own findings when he thinks the evidence he has turned up is insufficient for firm conclusions. Perhaps we may say that all thoughtful writing about legal government, regardless of its correspondence with what actually exists or occurs, is support for scientific investigation of legal government.

If the foregoing paragraph is read with approval, it becomes apparent that thoughtful students will disagree as to where to draw a line between scientific inquiry and inquiry that is not scientific but which provides support for the scientific inquiry. I shall not attempt to draw a line. I think it will be sufficient for our further discussion to identify certain types of study that seem clearly to pursue scientific method as I defined scientific method above; to give for each type of study some indication of what American political scientists have undertaken; and to note what progress we seem to have made in arriving at generalizations which contribute to a science of politics. This examination of our scientific endeavor will be arranged under four heads: (1) Description of Single Entities; (2) Comparative Description of Entities; (3) Variable Analysis; (4) Means to Ends Analysis.

DESCRIPTION OF SINGLE ENTITIES

Earlier in this essay I said that description is a report of what actually exists or occurs. By description of an entity, I mean description of something the writer conceives to be a

whole and differentiable from everything he does not conceive to be a part of this whole. I think we need not worry
about the sufficiency of these two sentences. It may be we
can never know (agree beyond likelihood of dispute) what
exists and occurs and therefore that we can never give a
wholly dependable report of what actually exists and occurs.
It may be that nothing can be differentiated from everything
else and therefore that all conceptions of entities are delu-
sions. We shall presume here that man can describe something man conceives to be an entity.

Scientific method fixes some standards for description of
an entity. In identifying something as an entity to be described, the student should exercise care and utilize existing
knowledge and belief in order to determine with assurance
that what he intends to embrace in his description is differentiable from what he does not intend to embrace in terms
of some test of significance. Having decided what he will
describe, his search for evidence should be comprehensive;
he should be imaginative in making decisions as to what is
relevant to and significant for his description. In the search
for evidence he should pursue methods which experience
and imaginative thought indicate are most likely to disclose
evidence and induce accurate observations. Evaluations of
evidence should be carefully made. And what is finally accepted as evidence should be fitted together with caution and
with imagination to provide the descriptive account which
will be made available to others.

Descriptions of single entities meeting the foregoing standards have three main significances for study that seeks to
build a science by establishing generalizations. (1) Isolated
descriptions inform the scientist. Scientists lay plans and
adopt strategies which promise to advance them most surely
and most rapidly toward generalizations. Careful accounts
of what life is like here and there disclose evidence that regularities may exist, therefore guide the scientist in formulat-

ing hypotheses, and tip him off as to where he may look with greatest hope of getting the additional evidence he needs. (2) Isolated descriptions which are not part of a planned search for generalizations may report findings that someday will be fitted together with other findings to support a generalization worthy of a place in scientific literature. Certainly some tentative generalizations (grand hypotheses) relating to natural phenomena have rested in part on findings reported in studies made without contemplation of the generalization that later emerged. It may be, however, that natural scientists will not consider the generalization sufficiently verified to stand as a scientific proposition until the finding is again reported by a student who designed his inquiry especially to test the proposed generalization. (3) The description of a single entity which is part of a strategic plan for arriving at or testing a generalization stands its greatest chance of finding a permanent place in an enduring literature of science. Whether it finds such a place will depend, of course, on the success of the general strategy of which it is a part, whether this particular report is later judged to be a critical part of the total body of findings resulting from the strategic plan, and whether the generalization arrived at or tested is later judged to be an important item in the literature of science.

At an earlier point (pp. 36–40) I tried to identify the main objects of description in the descriptive studies American political scientists carry on. Perhaps most of the descriptive studies we have made are properly classified as descriptions of single entities. I think the entities identified for separate description tend to be one of these: (a) a governmental-political system (e.g., Robert C. Brooks, *Government and Politics of Switzerland,* World Book, 1918; Robert B. Highsaw and Charles N. Fortenberry, *The Government and Administration of Mississippi,* Crowell, 1954); or (b) an institution (e.g., Ervin Hexner, *The International Steel Cartel,*

University of North Carolina, 1943; Byrum E. Carter, *The Office of Prime Minister*, Princeton University Press, 1956); or (c) an organization (e.g., the Brookings Institution monographs describing various departments and agencies of the United States national government); or (d) a way of doing something (e.g., Harold Kurtzman, *Methods of Controlling Votes in Philadelphia*, University of Pennsylvania, 1935; Murray Edelman, *The Licensing of Radio Services in the United States, 1927 to 1947*, University of Illinois Press, 1950); or (e) the performance of an act, making of a decision, or adoption of a policy (e.g., Stephen K. Bailey, *Congress Makes a Law*, Columbia University, 1949; the case studies in *Public Administration and Policy Development*, edited by Harold Stein, Harcourt, Brace, 1952); or (f) a policy or continued course of action in which legal government expresses its expectations of one or more publics (e.g., Paul M. Zeis, *American Shipping Policy*, Princeton University, 1938; Mulford Q. Sibley and Philip E. Jacob, *Conscription of Conscience: The American State and the Conscientious Objector, 1940–1947*, Cornell University, 1952).

After reviewing recent publications, examining numerous bibliographies, and consulting some of my colleagues, I reach the conclusion that until quite recently American political scientists have not been greatly concerned with providing descriptions of single entities that stand a good chance of entering into a scientific literature. It may be that most writing of this character which we have done will give aid to the scientific enterprise by suggesting what needs to be looked into or by indicating where certain kinds of evidence can be found. But I think it certain that few of these studies were specifically designed to produce findings that will add to others to produce a body of generalizations, and I think it unlikely that many contain findings that will by chance fit into the structure that produces a useful generalization. My general conclusion that most of these studies have either no value or low value for science is induced by these more limited conclusions:

(1) Most of our descriptive studies are casual in the search for evidence. Many of them may properly be called simple reporting of something that has occurred or something that has been created. The search for evidence stopped when the statutes and court decisions were read, when facts were gleaned from one or two newspapers, when the observations and opinions of a few leading participants were obtained; indeed, our journals carry many articles (and textbooks repeat the findings) which were written without the benefit of more than one of these limited sources of information.

(2) Many of our studies do not comprehend anywhere near everything that is relevant to and significant for understanding the entity the author promises to describe. Thus a study that purports to describe an organization may tell you where the statute or an organization chart says authority to make decisions lies, but the report does not tell you where in the organization decisions are actually made; or tell you what arrangements exist to bring to the attention of deciders the hopes and expectations of people who will be affected by the decision; or tell you how information and advice as to most effective means for achieving desired results flows to the men who make the decisions; or how instructions flow to the people who are expected to change their behavior because a new decision has been made. The search for evidence the author thought he needed may have been exemplary; what he thought he needed for a full description suffered from lack of imagination.

(3) Many of the descriptions we have produced were made in order to support a special purpose and not to provide information many students can use for many purposes. Examination of this part of our literature indicates that two special purposes have greatly affected what we embrace in our de-

scriptions: *First,* the author wishes to prove that a novelty or innovation has come into existence. He describes a newly created organization or a recently adopted policy or a distinctive way of doing something. The description he provides is not designed to disclose facts about this entity which will help us to understand what exists and occurs in other entities; rather it is designed to tell us what is particular to the entity he describes and so of least usefulness in guiding our study of other entities. *Second,* the author provides only that amount of description which seems needed to support an analysis or a critique he intends to make. The description he supplies may be the result of imaginative and careful search for evidence; it may comprehend everything needed as preparation for the analysis or critique which follows. But the value of the description is limited to the uses for which it was designed. The report of what actually exists and occurs is not sufficiently comprehensive to serve as a reservoir of knowledge which other students can tap in trying to find out what exists and occurs in a number of comparable entities. The consequences, for description, of a concern to make particular kinds of analysis were noted above (pp. 41–46) in the discussion of literature relating to constitutional law and the judicial process.

(4) Descriptive studies that meet stern requirements of scientific method are as yet too few to support much hope that the findings they report will ultimately add to other findings and so contribute to generalizations worthy of a place in scientific literature. My recent re-examination of our literature forces me to conclude that there are far fewer of them than I had previously supposed. A list of the best known and most highly regarded descriptive accounts by American political scientists would include, I suppose, John Gaus and Leon Wolcott, *Public Administration and the United States Department of Agriculture* (Public Administration Service, 1940); Arthur Macmahon, John Millett, and

Gladys Ogden, *The Administration of Federal Work Relief* (Public Administration Service, 1941); Charles Hardin, *Politics of Agriculture* (The Free Press, 1952); and the reports on enactment of legislation by E. E. Schattschneider, Stephen Bailey, Fred Riggs, and Earl Latham. American political scientists have produced few other descriptions of single entities which seem to me to match these in quality.

COMPARATIVE DESCRIPTION OF ENTITIES

On a test of ultimate contribution to a science, comparative descriptions of two or more entities appear to be an advance beyond descriptions of single entities. When one study embraces two or more entities of comparable character the same tests of relevance and significance can be applied to each entity and the descriptions which result can put a spotlight on likenesses and unlikenesses, on what the entities have in common and on respects in which they differ. As our knowledge of likenesses and differences is increased, we approach the point in study where generalized statements can be made.

A great deal of what was said above about descriptions of single entities is applicable to comparative descriptions. As one student is challenged to exercise care and utilize existing knowledge in identifying an entity for a one-case description, so another student is challenged to proceed both cautiously and imaginatively in choosing two or more entities suitable for the kinds of comparison he intends to make. (On this see the apt remarks of Herbert Simon in No. 63.) In comparative descriptions as in descriptions of single entities, the effort can fail because of inadequate comprehension of what is relevant and significant to the description or because the search for evidence is not sufficiently rigorous. The value for science of one-case descriptions is restricted by the special purposes for which the writers expected their descriptions to be used; there is reason to suppose that comparative descriptions will suffer even greater restrictions for this reason. As the number of entities increases, the range of matters relevant and significant for description increases and the obstacles encumbering the search for evidence grow in abundance. As the number of entities increases, the student brings to the study less of previously acquired familiarity with the universe he examines, and greater resources in time, energy, and investigative devices are required. These considerations are compulsions to which most students must yield, and the concession they make is a less comprehensive description of the phenomena, or a less rigorous search for evidence, or both. And in order to bring the task down to manageable size, they are likely to design a study which yields data helpful for a particular goal of comparative analysis but which is of little or no aid to students who have other goals in mind.

There are differences in style of comparative studies. Some may be called parallel descriptions; the author separately describes his individual cases and follows the separate descriptions by an analysis in which he notes likenesses and differences and endows them with significance. In other studies the descriptions of separate entities are merged and integrated and the author identifies and evaluates likenesses and differences as he goes forward with description.

The subject matter examined in comparative descriptions ranges from the most inclusive entities (national systems) to sharply restricted entities (e.g., small groups). Grand comparisons (e.g., of national systems) appear mainly in textbooks; comparative study of smaller units is likely to be cast in the form of variable analysis, reserved for separate treatment below. Comparative descriptions of national systems usually adhere to the style I call parallel description, though we have produced some textbooks which attempt to merge and integrate the several descriptions (e.g., Carl J.

Friedrich, *Constitutional Government and Democracy,*
Ginn, 1950; Daniel Wit, *Comparative Political Institutions,*
Holt, 1953). Unlike the predominant treatment of national
systems, textbooks describing American state governments
and American local governments regularly merge and integrate the descriptive accounts and comment on likenesses
and differences as they are turned up in the description.

Writings by American political scientists joining two or
more nation-states in a comparative description are limited
almost wholly to comparisons of entire national systems and
with few exceptions are on a level of generality we have come
to expect of textbooks. In a recent review of literature
available for the study of comparative public administration
(No. 48), Fred W. Riggs cites only three books written by
American political scientists: Leonard D. White, *Civil Service Abroad: Great Britain, Canada, France, Germany* (Mc-
Graw-Hill, 1935); Donald C. Stone and others, *National
Organization for the Conduct of Economic Development
Programs* (Brussels, IIAS, 1954); and Walter Sharp and
others, *National Administration and International Organization: A Comparative Study of Fourteen Countries* (Brussels, IIAS, 1951). I think it is fair to say that each of these
volumes was designed to advance lay understanding or to
implement policy decisions and not to provide knowledge
that would contribute to the generalizations necessary for a
science.

The meagerness of our study comparing national experiences in administration appears to be matched in other areas
that invite comparative studies. A group of political scientists who met in 1953 to consider problems in comparative
study of national systems reported that "The study of comparative politics has been primarily concerned thus far with
the study of the formal institutions of governments—particu-
larly the governments of Western Europe. It has been in this
sense not only parochial but also primarily descriptive and

formalistic" (No. 63). I conclude from a later report that there are but few probing comparative studies of even the formal institutions of governments (No. 9). The concern that caused these and other students of national systems to be convened, and thoughtful analysis coming out of their joint deliberations (Nos. 7c, 9, 28, 63, 64) suggest that comparative descriptions that cross national boundaries may appear more frequently in the near future, and that points of comparison may move from the more formal or legal apparatus to a wide range of phenomena heretofore ignored in our study. For further evidence of determination to inaugurate a new day in comparative description, see recent articles by Gabriel Almond (No. 65), Frederick Engelmann (No. 71), Leon Epstein (No. 107), Joseph LaPalombara (No. 111), Sigmund Neumann (No. 80), and Lucian Pye (No. 83).

Studies by American political scientists providing comparative descriptions of entities located within a single nation-state are confined almost wholly to experience in the United States. Classified as to object of attention, comparative studies of American experience to date fall mainly into two groups: (a) comparative descriptions of administrative organizations of the national government, and (b) descriptions which compare experience in several or all of the 48 states. Illustrative of the first group of studies are: Pendleton Herring, *Public Administration and the Public Interest* (McGraw-Hill, 1936); Arthur W. Macmahon and John D. Millett, *Federal Administrators* (Columbia University, 1939); Robert C. Cushman, *The Independent Regulatory Commissions* (Oxford, 1941).

Earlier descriptions comparing experience in different American states seem to have been confined in the main to administrative organizations, public policies, or the way in which certain problems were dealt with. Illustrating studies of these types are: James W. Fesler, *The Independence of State Regulatory Agencies* (Public Administration Service,

1942); Schuyler C. Wallace, *State Administrative Supervision over Cities in the United States* (Columbia University, 1928); Joseph P. Harris, *Election Administration in the United States* (Brookings Institution, 1934); V. O. Key, *The Administration of Federal Grants to States* (Public Administration Service, 1937); and in article length, Schuyler Wallace on law enforcement (No. 128), and Clarence A. Berdahl and Joseph R. Starr on legal status of parties (Nos. 11 and 57).

The present decade has witnessed notable developments in inquiry that utilizes data drawn from two or more of the American states. Studies taking the form of variable analysis (separately treated below) have increased in number, and studies more properly called comparative descriptions of entities have taken on new dimensions in what they comprehend or embrace, have pressed more deeply into experience for evidence relevant and significant to the object of description, and have been more exacting in the evaluation of evidences which are fitted together to form findings and conclusions. At least one study (V. O. Key, with the assistance of Alexander Heard, *Southern Politics in State and Nation*, Knopf, 1949) has been widely acclaimed a model in each of these respects. Other recent studies illustrating this new development are: V. O. Key, *American State Politics: An Introduction* (Knopf, 1956); Alexander Heard, *A Two Party South?* (University of North Carolina, 1952); John H. Fenton, *Politics in the Border States* (Hauser Press, 1957); and the five-volume study of selection of delegates to the national party conventions of 1952 sponsored by the American Political Science Association and directed by Paul T. David (Johns Hopkins, 1954).

The effort of American political scientists to illuminate their subject by comparative descriptions to date has scarcely touched cities, counties, and other units of local government in the United States. Textbooks and a survey of county government edited by Paul W. Wager (*County Government*

Across the Nation, University of North Carolina, 1950) call attention to the more readily observable likenesses and differences. The few studies of local governments within a particular state are in the main satisfied to state what law provides, note readily observable likenesses and differences in formal organization, and comment on more outstanding successes and failures in dealing with the problems local governments are expected to deal with. William Anderson made a classification and count of governmental jurisdictions throughout the United States (*The Units of Government in the United States,* Public Administration Service, 1949); Arthur W. Bromage provided a summary account of abandonments of the council-manager form of city government (*Manager Plan Abandonments,* National Municipal League, 1949); and Edwin O. Stene and George K. Floro made a fuller inquiry into reasons for abandoning that form of government in four cities (*Abandonments of the Manager Plan: A Study of Four Small Cities,* University of Kansas, 1953). Perhaps the political science profession can claim two books by Harold A. Stone, Don K. Price, and Kathryn H. Stone (*City-Manager Government in the United States* and *City-Manager Government in Nine Cities,* both Public Administration Service, 1940). American political scientists have made some studies of metropolitan areas in which comparative descriptions of the associated local governments are provided; these descriptions are in most cases limited to features, aspects, practices significant for a particular analysis and critique of intergovernmental relations.

My recent re-examination of our literature, coupled with my general recollections, identifies no study in which an American political scientist selected a sample of American cities, or counties, or other local government units and then attempted a comparative description both comprehensive and intensive of the entities included in the sample. Perhaps the nearest we have approached such a study is John F. Sly,

Town Government in Massachusetts (Harvard University Press, 1930). Sly's study is in large part survey, and where it goes beyond survey his attention is directed to only a few of the matters necessary to a comprehensive description. The comparative description of local governments is yet to be written which brings into the account a careful treatment of differences in density of population, orientation of population to one or more urban centers, orientation of population to party and degree of competition between party organizations, or any of a number of other matters affecting the character of local government in the United States.

The foregoing remarks about the paucity of comparative descriptions of local governments may be compared with the observations of three young men who recently subjected our local government literature to exceptionally imaginative, objective, and incisive evaluation: articles by R. T. Daland (No. 15), Lawrence Herson (No. 26), and Allan Richards (No. 98).

VARIABLE ANALYSIS

I choose the term variable analysis as a label for one kind of effort to determine what actually exists and occurs. Variable analysis attempts to find out the relationships existing among two or more factors that collectively contribute to or make up a whole. Variable analysis provides descriptions, for it is designed to yield information enabling the student to report what actually exists and occurs insofar as relationships among different factors (variables) is concerned.

Variables are factors that bear a non-constant relationship to the collectivity of which they are a part. Helium is a gaseous element. Its atomic structure is constant, never varying; if you managed to alter the atomic structure, helium would cease to exist and something else would come into existence. But the space occupied by a given number of helium particles (volume) does vary as heat and pressure are applied. If you hold pressure constant and increase heat, volume increases; if you hold heat constant and increase pressure, volume decreases; if you hold volume constant and increase either heat or pressure, the other of these latter two qualities changes also. The description of a single helium particle is simplified by its fixed atomic structure. But a description of a number of helium particles viewed as a collectivity requires that one bring into the account measures of heat, of pressure, and of volume; the description of the collectivity is different as any of these factors (variables) are found to be different.

Things which political scientists describe (institutions, organizations, etc.) are collectivities made up of components varying in their relationships to one another. The office of mayor in the city called Bigtown is a collectivity which can be broken down into components including the legal endowments of the office, the personal characteristics and qualities of the man occupying the office, the goals and aggressiveness of members of the city council, the expectations and activities of party leaders, and so on almost ad infinitum if you press analysis to points of great precision. The office of mayor of Bigtown changes over periods of time for two reasons. (1) Each of these components, viewed as a separate entity, varies. The legal endowments of the office are changed; the personal characteristics and qualities of the incumbent of the office vary as different men are put in the office; and so on. (2) The pattern of relationships among the many components varies. While the legal endowments of the office remain constant, different men occupy the office; while both legal endowments and incumbency of the office remain constant, the city council becomes more aggressive or less aggressive in restraining the efforts of the incumbent mayor to do what he tries to do. The goal of variable analysis as applied to the office of mayor of Bigtown is (a) to identify the components (factors) associated together to make the office what it is at any given time, (b) to find out how these components are related so as to make the office what it is at any given time, and (c) to find out how the office changes as individual components vary and as relationships among the components vary. Obviously the accomplishment of this three-part goal poses difficulties of great magnitude. The difficulties compound if the collectivity to be studied is extended to include not only the office of mayor of Bigtown but the office of mayor in a sample of cities differing in size of population, legal endowments of the offices, party organization and activity, state of civic participation, and so on.

The economy achieved by study that determines relationships among variables is readily apparent. When manufacturers of equipment became confident, as a result of studies which produced the same findings, that applications of heat and pressure to gases have predictable consequences for volume, it became unnecessary to make tentative constructions and then test to determine their adequacy under different conditions of heat and pressure. Specific questions were answered by application of the verified generalizations. The goal of variable analysis applied to human relationships, including institutions like the office of mayor, is the identification of dependable relationships that can be expressed in generalized statements. It may well be the case that the zone of confident predictions is destined to be narrowly restricted in matters which political scientists study. But it may also be the case that variables which make up the collectivities we study are associated together in fairly persistent configurations. If persistent configurations do exist and we succeed in identifying them, this new knowledge can surely be expected to guide us more directly and with less expenditure of effort to the more specific knowledge we want about particular institutions and ways of doing things.

Studies I have classified as description of single entities and comparative descriptions of two or more entities are, at the least, helpful antecedents of variable analysis. The careful description of the office of mayor in one city, describing that office as of a given time, identifies many of the components another student will treat as variables and provides some knowledge about how these components support one another in making the office what it is. Perhaps all one-case descriptions we consider thoughtful provide information about changing relationships among components and about the consequences of such change for the character of the entity described. Comparative descriptions, of course, become significant for scholarship only if they show how differences in particular items contribute to differences in the collectivities that are objects of the study. Variable analysis is not a special kind of study sharply differentiable from elaborate descriptions of the types discussed above. Variable analysis is a term I use to identify studies in which attention to variables does not stop with their identification but goes beyond that point at least to find out with some precision how they unite at one time to form a whole and, in cases of more sophisticated analysis, to find out how changes in the relationships among variables affect the character of the collectivity of which they are a part. If any reader of this essay contends that V. O. Key's *Southern Politics,* which I cited as comparative description, is better classified as variable analysis, I shall not dispute his contention.

Studies by American political scientists that are most conscious of variables have been concerned mainly with voting in public elections, voting in legislative assemblies, and a variety of matters commonly labelled public opinion. The models for such studies were set for us by persons commonly not thought of as political scientists, and it may be that the most significant treatment of variables in these areas of study is still being done by persons not in political science departments. Prominent in this category of students are Louis

Bean, Bernard Berelson, Angus Campbell, Hadley Cantril, Leonard Doob, Paul Lazarsfeld, Samuel Lubell, and Stuart Rice. Political scientists have shared in this kind of study from an early date; among those who published significant studies before World War II are Ben A. Arneson, Herman C. Beyle, Harwood Childs, Cortez A. M. Ewing, Harold F. Gosnell, Donald Hecock, Arthur N. Holcombe, Harold Lasswell, A. Lawrence Lowell, Roscoe C. Martin, Charles E. Merriam, James K. Pollock, and Charles H. Titus.

Studies by American political scientists since World War II which relate to voting in public elections and which are most concerned with treatment of variables seem to be directed to three main points of attention. (1) Tendency of the electorate to vote or not to vote (turnout or participation) is made the dependent variable and the author seeks to find the relation to turnout of certain groupings of voters (independent variables) identified in terms of social indices (e.g., income class, age group, religious affiliation) or environmental conditions (e.g., urban-rural location, degree of party competition in the electoral jurisdiction. (2) Attachment of voters to a party or to a policy or program or to a leader or leaders is the dependent variable and groupings according to social indices and environmental conditions are independent variables. (3) Tendency to contest for public office is the dependent variable and environmental conditions (especially degrees of party competition in the electoral jurisdiction) are independent variables.

Data utilized in voting studies are predominantly of two kinds: (1) gross numerical data obtained from printed election returns and census publications; and (2) information disclosed in questionnaires and interviews. Objectives of inquiry, methods in collecting information, and problems encountered in analyzing data relating to voting in public elections are thoughtfully discussed in the items by Lindzey, Rossi, Eldersveld, Miller, and de Grazia cited above at p. 74.

Two books by V. O. Key cited above, *Southern Politics* and *American State Politics,* are directed to all three of the above-mentioned points of attention. Most fully explored are the first and second points of attention—turnout at the polls and attachment to party, policy or program, or leaders. Our knowledge of these matters has been enormously advanced since World War II by an intensive study of voting in Elmira, New York, and a series of publications using data sampling the electorate of the whole nation which was collected by the Survey Research Center of the University of Michigan in connection with the presidential elections of 1948 and 1952. Men trained in psychology and sociology were highly influential in planning and executing the search for data in these two cases, but political scientists shared in each enterprise and much of the analysis utilizing the Survey Research Center data is in publications authored by political scientists. The Elmira study is by Bernard R. Berelson, Paul F. Lazarsfeld, and William N. McPhee, *Voting: A Study of Opinion Formation in a Presidential Campaign* (University of Chicago, 1954). At least three monographs and more than a dozen articles have been based on the Survey Research Center data. The monographs are Angus Campbell and R. L. Kahn, *The People Elect a President* (University of Michigan, 1952); Angus Campbell, Gerald Gurin, and Warren Miller, *The Voter Decides* (Row, Peterson, 1954); and Morris Janowitz and Dwaine Marvick, *Competitive Pressure and Democratic Consent* (University of Michigan, 1956). Articles in the *American Political Science Review* which make use of Survey Research Center data appear in the list of references at the end of this essay (Nos. 12, 13, 16, 18, 19, 34, 42, 43, 58).

Independent of the Survey Research Center's collection of data are Lawrence H. Fuchs, *The Political Behavior of American Jews* (The Free Press, 1956); Malcolm Moos, *Politics, Presidents, and Coattails* (Johns Hopkins, 1952) examining attachment to party in elections of different officials; two studies of voting behavior in New Orleans—Leonard Reissmann, K. H. Silvert, and Cliff W. Wing, *The New Orleans Voter,* and Kenneth N. Vines, *Republicanism in New Orleans* (both in Vol. 2, "Tulane Studies in Political Science," Tulane University, 1955); a few pamphlet-sized studies illustrated by Ralph H. Smuckler and George M. Belknap, *Leadership and Participation in Urban Political Affairs* (Michigan State University, 1956); and a substantial number of articles in the *American Political Science Review, Public Opinion Quarterly,* and other journals.

Focusing on the third point of attention cited above—contesting for public office—in addition to the writings by Key, are Cortez A. M. Ewing, *Primary Elections in the South* (University of Oklahoma, 1953), and an article by Julius Turner on the relation of intensity of party competition in electoral jurisdictions to contests in direct primary elections (No. 88).

What has just been said should make it clear that American political scientists have already made substantial contributions to study of voting in public elections which takes the form I have called variable analysis. They have also contributed importantly to examination of variables that figure in the phenomena embraced in public opinion and communications study. Notable items appearing in the past decade include Gabriel A. Almond, *The American People and Foreign Policy* (Harcourt, Brace, 1950); and a series of monographs by Harold D. Lasswell, Daniel Lerner, Ithiel de Sola Pool, and others, which are generally identified as *Revolution and the Development of International Relations* ("Hoover Institute Studies," Stanford University, 1951 and later). The initial publications in the latter group are reviewed in *American Political Science Review,* Vol. 46 (1952), 867, 869. Considerable progress has also been made in study of voting in legislative assemblies. The United

States Congress was brought under examination by George
L. Grassmuck, *Sectional Biases in Congress on Foreign
Policy* (Johns Hopkins, 1951); and Julius Turner, *Party and
Constituency: Pressures on Congress* (Johns Hopkins, 1952);
and in shorter studies illustrated by the articles of Charles D.
Farris (No. 72), William H. Riker (No. 49), and David B.
Truman (No. 60). Analysis of voting behavior in American
state legislative assemblies has been advanced recently in a
number of articles by William Keefe (Nos. 30 and 110; see
also No. 2 at p. 308), Duane Lockard (No. 37), Malcolm
Jewell (No. 27), and Duncan MacRae (No. 39), and in
pamphlet-sized study by Murray C. Havens, *City* versus
Farm (University of Alabama, 1957). Finally, it may be noted
that American political scientists have recently resumed the
effort at content analysis which Lasswell and others pio-
neered several years ago (see No. 47 by James Prothro and
No. 41 by Roger H. Marz) and have pushed quantitative
study of judicial action considerably beyond the point to
which it was previously carried by Beyle and Pritchett (see
Kort in No. 32 and the discussion of his method in Nos. 22
and 33).

To date, variable analysis has been restricted in the main
to matters for which precise information is available—election figures, other data expressed in numbers, and disclosures
in questionnaires and interviews. It appears feasible to identify larger items that are components of a still greater collectivity, treat these components as variables, and so carry
analysis of the type I have been discussing into subject
matter areas as yet explored only by less precise methods.
The examination of the office of mayor imagined above (pp.
93–94) suggests what we would encounter if we attempted
to apply variable analysis to more inclusive entities. I understand political scientists were advised to make just such a
venture by a small group who met in 1951 to explore objectives and methods in research relating to political be-

havior (No. 64), and it may be that similar advice is intended in a recent article by Oliver Garceau (No. 23) and a more recent lecture by David Truman (No. 4 at p. 202). The advice is given, of course, because the kind of study I have called variable analysis is thought to offer real promise of leading us to generalizations about institutions and about behavior which, in turn, will guide us most surely and with least expenditure of effort to the more particular knowledge political scientists and other consumers of our product seek to obtain.

We must be prepared to meet several exacting requirements if we intend to travel this road with hope of success at the end. We must define precisely the collectivities we study and the individual components or factors we treat as variables. We must develop theories about relationships among variables and formulate hypotheses that direct search for evidence which is needed and which can be found. We must temper imagination with caution in evaluating items of evidence and fitting items together into findings and conclusions. And we must withstand the temptation to announce generalizations before we have examined enough experience to justify conclusion that further findings will not run counter to the findings we have made to date. For a statement of what the requirements are and counsel about how to go about meeting them, see a recent article by Avery Leiserson (No. 112).

MEANS TO ENDS ANALYSIS

We may presume that a society which maintains a discipline for pursuit of scholarly study expects that discipline to pay off sooner or later in knowledge that can be used in attaining what the society views as the good life. A discipline that is wholly concerned with building a science defers the payoff to a late date. It promises richer rewards in the end if society will wait until generalizations have been established, for the generalizations are take-off points for quick and sure advance to specific knowledge society can make use of. Many American political scientists think that their discipline ought to make substantial payments to society right now. Some of them, no doubt, fear that society will not continue to support us if all we deliver is promise of useful knowledge at some future time; others, no doubt, are skeptical that we will ever produce generalizations that constitute a science of politics.

Political scientists have followed a pay-in-part-as-you-go policy ever since they emerged as a separate discipline. Certain forms of payment were discussed in Chapter I of this essay—bringing our expertise to public affairs, training for the public service, and so on. We also offer immediate payments in our scholarly literature. Many of the books we write are addressed to an audience of political and civic leaders and lay citizens. Many of the articles we put in journals circulating mainly to members of our profession carry findings of immediate interest to the general public and offer advice the author hopes public leaders will follow in running the government. Whether because they think political scientists ought to, or only because they think political scientists will continue to, offer advice to leaders and lay public, many political scientists are now urging the profession to get busy at more systematic study of issues and problems of current public concern. Perhaps most attention has been given to Harold Lasswell's recommendations for development of what he calls policy sciences (No. 3, chapter 1, No. 35, and No. 36).

Writing by political scientists about public policy may place emphasis on the desirability of achieving certain goals, or it may place emphasis on ways and means of achieving certain goals. Differentiation of the two kinds of emphasis is difficult in some writings, for the goal which the author says is socially desirable may be supported by an argument that it is an effective means for achieving another goal which society or some part of society seems determined to attain. Acknowledging difficulty in assigning particular writings to one category or the other, we shall reserve for later treatment literature in which recommended policies or actions are largely supported by statements of the writer's personal preferences and convictions. At this point we shall give attention to study which, by search for persuasive evidence, attempts to determine how specified ends may be effectively achieved.

A review of literature produced by American political scientists over many decades establishes beyond doubt that finding out how social ends can be achieved has long been a prime preoccupation of the profession. I suggested above (pp. 83–86) that our descriptions of single entities have limited value for science because the descriptions are developed to support a particular critique or analysis which the author intends to make. I think it probable that in most cases the critique or analysis which the description supports is concerned with relationships between means and ends. To illustrate: the writer supposes (he may attempt to establish by evidence) that a public desires certain kinds of performance by legislative bodies; he describes a unicameral legislature or a bicameral legislature or a committee system or a set of relationships between executive and legislature and uses the description to support statements that the public is getting or not getting the kinds of performance it wants from the set of arrangements and relationships he has described; he offers advice as to what changes in arrangements and relationships are likely to lead to more satisfactory performance. If, in order to bring a greater amount of experience into the descriptive account, the author undertakes a comparative description, in this case also the description is usually designed to support judgments about how effectively the things that are described serve as means for achieving certain ends and to support speculation about other arrangements and relationships more likely to assure attainment of the ends which are in mind.

There can be no question that the literature describing American government—national, state, and local—is heavy with judgments about the consequences of organizations, arrangements, and practices for accomplishment of the purposes for which these governments were set up. I am told that the literature describing international organizations and practices is greatly concerned with the relationships of organizations and practices to the settlement of particular disputes or the avoidance of war. A like concern about means to ends is apparent in much of the literature which subordinates description of what exists and occurs and which develops extensively the author's ideas and beliefs; the author's ideas and beliefs are revealed in statements that contemporary institutions and ways of doing things do not yield the results that society or particular publics anticipated and with recommendations of ways and means of moving more effectively toward social goals. In contrast to these categories of literature, a great proportion of the writing that is most concerned with establishing relationships among components of collectivities—what I have called variable analysis—is likely to carry no comment about how effective the matters described are for achieving desired ends or about alternative arrangements and practices which might be more effective.

The dissatisfaction with present effort which causes some political scientists to recommend a reorientation to policy science arises not from belief that we ignore issues of current public concern but from belief that we can provide better analysis than we have been providing. Much of our writing which, in the view of one man, offers evidence or convincing argument that certain arrangements and practices are effective means to an end is, in another man's view, inadequate evidence or argument because the author did not establish that the means played a critical role in accomplishment of the end and that alternative means would not have contributed as effectively to attainment of the end. The call for political scientists to turn their attention to means-ends analysis is less a challenge to replace the goals that presently determine what we inquire into than it is a challenge to improve the quality of the inquiries we make.

Descriptions of successful and unsuccessful experiments are first steps toward means-ends analysis. The first description of a city's council-manager government gives an account of what people in one community conceived and were willing to try out, and perhaps adds statements about why those people thought the new experiment would satisfy them better than what they had previously had. A later description of the same experiment reports the relationships that have actually developed among the people who constitute the government, gives an account of things tried and found satisfactory and things tried but abandoned, and perhaps adds statements about public content and discontent with the experiment to date. These descriptions, both the account of what is intended and the account of what has happened, are of value to people in other places. They direct imagination to what can be done and fix points on which many people can focus attention in speculating about what might happen if they created a similar governmental structure in their community. The description of one successful experiment does not prove that nothing else would have been satisfactory if it had been tried, and does not prove that an effort to duplicate it will prove satisfactory to another community. The value of the description lies in its appeal to the imagination; those who read the description call to mind their own observations and experience and assume the risk involved if they decide to create a council-manager government for their own city.

The comparative description of several council-manager

governments, if elaborate and carefully made, provides fuller support for judgments and assumptions of risk in altering governmental structure. If it reveals that in all cities where the council is elected by party ballot the discretion of managers is narrowly confined and administration of public services is generally unsatisfactory, and that the opposite is the case in all cities where the council is elected by non-partisan ballot, the description warns people to ponder carefully methods of electing the council before they fix the design for the council-manager government they intend to establish. But the coincidence of successes and failures with different methods of balloting is not conclusive evidence that success or failure turns on the form of the ballot. One needs to know whether successes and failures coincide only with different forms of ballot, or coincide also with other devices or social conditions. Further extension of the inquiry might reveal that satisfactions and dissatisfactions with public services are coincident with different states of civic organization and with orientations of the population to community enterprise and so introduce doubt that either the discretion granted to the manager or the method of electing the council accounts for the character of administrative services or popular reactions to them.

Greatest hope of identifying the means which offer highest assurance of contributing to specified ends, in the view of many political scientists, is what I have called variable analysis. At risk of misrepresenting them, I suggest that these political scientists would justify their conviction in this manner. Any problem of ascertaining or designing means to ends which requires the attention of a learned discipline brings the student face to face with a large number of items bearing unknown relationships to one another. If the problem is to be resolved by research and thoughtful speculation, the student must examine experience which his present state of knowledge, mobilized and ordered by imagination, tells

him is most likely to provide clues to the additional knowledge he seeks. Let us presume that he decides to examine two
experiments—one a successful effort and one an unsuccessful
effort to achieve the end with which he is concerned. He must
identify everything (items which he calls variables) he thinks
most likely to have contributed to the successful and to the
unsuccessful effort to achieve the end. Having identified the
supposedly relevant items, he must determine how they were
related to one another in the two experiments which he examines. If the examination reveals significant differences in
the way the items were related to one another in the two
situations, he may think he is justified in stating a pattern of
relationships most likely, in new experiments, to result in
achievement of the desired ends. If examination of the two
experiments does not give him all the knowledge he thinks
he needs for venturing a prediction as to what will work in
new experiments, he may extend his attention to additional
items (variables) not considered in his first examination, or
he may bring additional successes and failures under scrutiny. A study conducted in this fashion is a pursuit of variable analysis.

If what I have said up to this point is both sound and
sufficient, one is led up to a conclusion that means-ends
analysis does not call for methods of study different from
those discussed above under the heads: description of single
entities, comparative description of entities, and variable
analysis. Indeed, I think it likely that all political scientists
who urge a vigorous development of policy sciences would
recommend continued pursuit of each of the three types of
inquiry. The significant implications of the proposal that
political scientists get ahead with means to ends analysis
(develop a policy science) relate to (1) what we select as
objects of attention in particular inquiries; (2) the adequacy
of research designs and procedures for getting the informa-

tion we need; and (3) the presentations we make when we have completed our searches and analyses.

I have already noted my belief that much of our study in the past and at present has been and is directed to objects of attention suitable for careful means to ends analysis. It may be that the presentation of our findings and judgments suffers from ambivalence in identification of the audience most interested in what we have to report—that we put in journals which circulate to a scholarly audience descriptions, analyses, and argumentations which add little or nothing to the scholar's stock of knowledge but which, if distributed through other channels, would have great suggestive value to publics having responsibility for decisions and actions. Whatever may be warranted conclusions on these points, it cannot be denied that those who currently challenge us to vigorous development of a policy science insist that political scientists show greater ingenuity in design of research, direct more imagination and devote more energy to search for evidence, and exercise more caution than has usually been displayed in fitting evidence into findings and fitting findings into conclusions about how ends may be effectively achieved.

A final point implied in what has already been said may be worthy of express statement. A decision of political scientists to supply a public need for means to ends analysis is not incompatible with a determination to establish generalizations that contribute to a science of politics. As descriptions of single entities may provide findings that by chance can be assimilated with other findings to form bases for generalizations, so the findings resulting from any style of means-ends analysis may by chance support generalizations of highest significance. Furthermore, a commitment to means-ends analysis does not force one to concentrate on studies that pay off immediately in advice to deciding and acting publics; the search for effective means may proceed in a roundabout way that first establishes generalizations and later takes off from generalizations to establish most effective means for achieving specified ends. The admiration which has so generally been expressed for Harold Gosnell's *Getting Out the Vote* (University of Chicago, 1927) offers sufficient proof that one study can both advance us toward generalizations and give sound advice about ways and means of arriving at a desired objective.

CHAPTER VI

Normative Doctrine and Proposals
for Social Action

We now direct attention to literature produced by American political scientists which falls in the last of the four categories adopted for this analysis. We are concerned now with writing which announces and develops the author's personal position.

PERSONAL POSITION: ENDS AND MEANS

Writings which present the author's personal position have two major points of emphasis. They may be directed (1) to aggrandizement of particular values or a value system which the author personally subscribes to, or (2) to presentation of the author's personal convictions about suitable means for accomplishing particular ends in instances where evidence from experience is insufficient to establish the most effective means for achieving those ends. For convenience in expression, I shall hereafter refer to the first point of emphasis as personal preference, to the second point of emphasis as personal conviction; when both are included in my reference, I shall say personal position.

The differentiation I make between two major points of

emphasis may appear to some readers unwarranted. I recognize that risk is involved in making classifications that turn on differentiation of means from ends. I find classification on this basis useful in examining our literature, even though I recognize that ends and means are merely points on a continuum. At one end of the continuum are suppositions about that which is good for its own sake, identifications of ends that provide their own justification. I think we may properly call these esthetic values. Not far removed from these identifications are some others that I shall call mixed means-ends suppositions; concerning these, one is often not clear whether he regards them as esthetic values (ends that provide their own justification) or whether he regards them as means that directly or indirectly contribute to esthetic values. Freedom of expression illustrates. Often one cannot tell whether a writer considers free choice in expression to be an end that is sufficiently justified by the fact that men like to say what they choose to say, or considers free choice in expression to be a means justified only by its utility in enabling men to control their government or to maximize their income or to defend some other interest which the author conceives to be an end. Still further on the continuum are things that are valued solely because they contribute to other more highly valued matters; these things are viewed as effective means for achieving ends that, in turn, may be either esthetic values or only means to still other ends.

It happens that I find persuasive the argument that nothing can provide its whole justification; I find attractive the supposition that the mind can fix a value for any matter only by observing how that matter supports or inhibits realization of other matters that tentatively appear to have value because they in turn bear certain relations to other matters. Taking this view, I presume that what one man, after searching scrutiny, identifies as an esthetic value becomes for me at best a mixed means-ends proposition. Agreement on clas-

sification is not required for pursuit of the analysis of literature that follows, however; I note my own position only to
make evident my appreciation of the difficulties one encounters in examining a literature in which statements about
preferred values and statements of personal conviction about
suitable means to ends are prominent.

The term "personal position" suggests preference or conviction which is peculiar to the author of the particular
writing in which the position is revealed. It should be noted
that many statements of preference and conviction represent
a position common to many members of the discipline.
When substantial numbers of men in any discipline reveal
a common position in their writings, the literature they
produce, if influential on any public, may have consequences
that other members of the discipline greatly deplore. The
great preoccupation of textbooks on American government
a few years back with venality and stupidity of public officials
must have had an effect on evaluations of the American
political system by college students which was not wholly
erased by occasional *caveats* that more good men than bad
men hold high offices. A concurrence in emphasis on the part
of those who write on the subject that widely shared values,
commitments, and convictions (labelled conformity) stifle
inventiveness, innovation, and individual self-expression (labelled liberty) may cause those who are impressed by this
literature to underestimate the role of conformity in establishing community and making cooperative effort possible.
Selective rather than comprehensive attention to evidence
and partial rather than comprehensive and exhaustive analysis in studies of national-state-local governmental relations
may create or bolster suppositions that satisfaction with governmental policies and services is the only test that need be
applied to the distribution of power between levels of government and induce an undervaluation of the significance
of different levels of government for the political organiza-

tion and politicking that make popular control of government effective. On the bias resulting from common position, see No. 77.

Writings by American political scientists which claim a place in scholarly literature and which rest that claim in large part on statements of personal position fall roughly into two categories and will be examined here under two heads: Normative Doctrine and Proposals for Social Action. This division conforms to the two points of emphasis identified at the beginning of this section, aggrandizement of values and presentation of personal conviction about suitable means to ends. Differentiations of literature for assignment to these two headings in many instances will be arbitrary. If the discourse is mainly directed to values or ends and is relevant to individual or group commitment, the item will be cited as normative doctrine. If, however, the author puts emphasis on social instruments for achieving ends and on recommendations for continuance of existing instruments, modification of these instruments, or adoption of new ones—in such cases his contribution will be considered under the second head, Proposals for Social Action. It may be that most items which clearly fall under one head are just as properly treated under the other because the author has a dual purpose—to win acceptance of an end and to encourage action designed to achieve that end. Furthermore, many items of literature defy classification. The author leaves too much for the reader to guess. He may cite an end, acknowledge or not acknowledge his own commitment, offer no argumentation or obviously inadequate argumentation as to why the reader should make a similar commitment and shape his conduct accordingly. He may propose social action, arguing for continuance of the status quo or making a case for change in social instruments, but leave the reader in doubt as to what ends he wishes to see advanced by the social program he endorses. I shall be content if, in the pages which follow, I adequately indicate the character of the writing we do; I shall not be disturbed by charges of poor judgment in assigning items of literature to one or the other of the two heads.

NORMATIVE DOCTRINE

There appears to be general agreement among American political scientists that their assignment includes analysis and criticism of statements about values found in literature, in ideologies, and in other evidences of public position. At least a substantial number of American political scientists have indicated a belief that political scientists should also formulate, develop, and support by argumentation statements about values which represent their own preferences.

Harry Eckstein reports (No. 17, at p. 486) that the "anti-behaviorists" participating in a recent conference on the relation of political theory to the study of politics announced as one of two tasks for the political scientist: "First, he should undertake the never-ending task of ethical and moral reflection: ethical reflection toward the definition and critique of ultimate imperatives, moral reflection toward the definition of actions which can approach the imperatives in practical activity. In effect, he should address himself to the matter of ends and means, to the problems of choice in practical activity rather than the analysis of behavior as a given. His function, in this sense, is to be a source of directives for society in general."

A major point in David Easton's article on the decline of modern political theory (No. 68), restated less fully in his *The Political System,* is that American political scientists have not made notable additions to value theory. Value theory, he says (p. 38 of the article), "refers not to what *is* but to the state of affairs that men would like to see come into existence. They are consciously value-oriented statements. They describe the way in which the desired social order should be organized, if the values adopted by the theorists are to be realized." Value theory, he continues, embraces three kinds of propositions, one of which "implies the choice of a constellation of values or preferences which the political theorist uses as a criterion to appraise social policy." Later in the same article (p. 48) he adds: "My point is that the enterprise of defining the situation in evaluational terms is a legitimate one for the political theorist because as a social scientist, he is in close touch with the data of empirical relations, and as a value theorist, he is directly involved with human goals." A reading of the article as a whole leads to the conclusion that Easton thinks the construction of value theory not simply legitimate for the political theorist but an essential task for some members of the discipline we call political science. Further, as noted above (p. 61) Easton concludes that we are not discharging this obligation adequately and offers his explanation of why we fail. I understand that Benjamin Lippincott, also quoted above (pp. 61–62), shares Easton's conclusion about inadequate performance and Easton's explanation of why we fail to meet an obligation.

What Eckstein appears to mean by "ethical reflection toward the definition and critique of ultimate imperatives" and what Easton calls value theory, I intend to embrace under the term normative doctrine. If the author identifies an end which seems to him to provide its own justification, makes clear what he is talking about, makes an appeal for others to commit themselves to the end he poses—such writing is a prime example of normative doctrine.

Landon Rockwell (No. 50 at pp. 316–17) indicates some of the central points of concern in normative doctrine. He says that the subject matter of analysis by political scientists has five components, one of which is political ideas. Political ideas, in some instances, he says, "are motivating forces; at least they explain motivating forces. They probably have the greatest survival value and power, for they deal with the great themes of human striving: justice, liberty, consent, equality, toleration, power, authority, security, welfare. And because of this they are basic to any systematic, rational approach to the political process." We may view, I think, as model efforts to develop normative doctrine, St. Augustine and St. Thomas on justice, authority, and law; Locke on toleration; Rousseau on equality; Mill on liberty.

The literature produced by American political scientists does not include many items that frankly announce as the central point of concern the author's preference among alternative values, seek to justify or explain the choice, and make an appeal for others to commit themselves to the same choice. I cannot identify for an American political scientist a personal testament comparable to David Lilienthal's *This I Do Believe,* a statement that is essentially autobiographical, offered for no purpose other than to give other people whatever benefit they may derive from learning what the author has arrived at, how he reached his position, why he likes what he likes or believes what he believes. The following are among the best examples I have found of effort to make a forthright presentation of normative doctrine by persons I understand to be American political scientists: Paul H. Appleby, *Morality and Administration in Democratic Government* (Louisiana State University, 1952); George A. Graham, *Morality in American Politics* (Random House, 1952); Dorothy Fosdick, *Common Sense and World Affairs* (Harcourt, Brace, 1955); Charles B. Marshall, *The Limits of Foreign Policy* (Holt, 1954); Walter Berns, *Freedom, Virtue and the First Amendment* (Louisiana State University, 1957).

By far the greatest part of the writing by our profession which sets forth normative doctrine has a purpose other than statement of the author's personal preference. Usually the other purpose is given greatest prominence; statements of preference and appeals to commitment are made to appear secondary. Two purposes predominate: (1) analysis and critique of ideas developed by persons other than the author, and (2) descriptions of real situations. In many writings both of these purposes are apparent. The author describes something that exists and occurs, he examines ideas relating to what he has described, and he supplies by implication or open avowal his own preferences among values or ends that are at stake in what he describes.

It follows that writings which are noteworthy for presentation of personal position cannot be sharply differentiated from literature which earlier in this essay was typed as descriptive writing or as examination of ideas. Selections of items for citation in the remaining pages of this chapter are therefore arbitrary. Some that are cited below were also cited earlier as descriptions or examinations of ideas; perhaps all that are cited below were appropriate for citation above.

1. Analysis and Critique of Ideas

Writings that seek to provide objective critical analysis and evaluation of value positions observed in publics or found in the writings of other people may make important contributions to normative doctrine. The critical treatment, if done with distinction, reduces the appeal of normative doctrine that does not stand up under criticism, and gives new impetus and added strength to doctrine that is found sufficient and persuasive. Furthermore, in many cases assertions and implications of approval and disapproval make obvious to the reader the preferences of a writer who announces a wish to be read only as an analyst. In other cases, where greatest effort is made to avoid statements and implications of preference, the value holdings of the analyst are made apparent by the character of his criticism and the development of his argumentation. Most readily perceived as contribution to normative doctrine, no doubt, is the document in which the author frankly and carefully states his own value position and does the best he knows how to make it attractive to skeptical readers.

Much of our writing that is significant for normative doctrine offers critical analysis and evaluation of value implications, readily apparent or hidden, in governmental policies, pronouncements and acts of public officials, and statements of political leaders. Perhaps most critical examinations of judicial decisions and other governmental actions affecting the status of individuals have significance for normative doctrine. Illustrative, and differing as to prominence of the author's value position, are: The book by Berns cited above (p. 115); Robert K. Carr, *Federal Protection of Civil Rights; Quest for a Sword* (Cornell University, 1947); C. Herman Pritchett, *Civil Liberties and the Vinson Court* (University of Chicago, 1954); and three recent articles in *Journal of Politics* by Wallace Mendelson (No. 79), Earl Latham (No. 76), and Loren P. Beth (No. 67). Examining value holdings of great publics as well as value positions revealed in public policy are: Westel W. Willoughby, *Prussian Political Philosophy* (Appleton, 1918); Louis C. Kesselman, *The Social Politics of FEPC* (University of North Carolina, 1948); Thomas I. Cook and Malcolm Moos, *Power through Purpose; The Realism of Idealism as a Basis for Foreign Policy* (Johns Hopkins, 1954); and Morton Grodzins, *The Loyal and the Disloyal* (University of Chicago, 1956). Starting with value propositions highly developed in literature but marked sufficiently by the author's value holdings to make them original contributions to normative doctrine are: Westel W. Willoughby, *The Ethical Basis of Political Authority* (Macmillan, 1930); John H. Herz, *Political Realism and Political Idealism* (University of Chicago, 1951); Francis G. Wilson, *The Case for Conservatism* (University of Washington, 1951); and articles by Cecilia M. Kenyon on controlling government (No. 31), Currin V. Shields on collectivism (No. 53), David Spitz on civil disobedience (No. 56), J. Roland

Pennock on free speech (No. 119), and Robert G. McCloskey on conservatism and democracy (No. 114).

2. Descriptions of Real Situations

Preference of the author for particular values also comes out in studies that are primarily designed to provide accounts of what actually exists and occurs. Perhaps most studies of which this is true have as their objects of description problems and issues confronting governments or public officials, public policies, significant acts of public officials or attitudes and conduct of public officials, or events and occurrences having significance for legal governments. Value positions can readily be identified in the real situations which are described, whether national governments or international associations are involved. Perhaps in most cases alternative value systems are in sharp competition for domination. What happens in these situations is determined in large part by the value holdings and commitments of various publics, and equally, what happens in these situations has an impact on the values held by publics, on individual and group commitments, and possibly on personal conduct. The value implications of any such situation must of necessity be prominently featured in a thoroughgoing descriptive account.

It is probable that most students who undertake descriptions of such matters as are mentioned in the preceding paragraph are attracted to the job because of personal interest in the value issues at stake. Certainly many descriptive accounts which purport to be objective statements of what exists and occurs are marked by obvious evidences of the author's preferences. Even in cases where the author seeks most faithfully to achieve and maintain objectivity, analysis may be influenced by his preferences. Descriptions of value-laden situations, even where the author's preferences are most subdued, have impact on the value positions of others;

those who trust the account find confirmation for their existing commitments or are challenged to reconsider their commitments. If the author's preferences are unleashed and he constructs his account in such a way that what he likes wins the sympathy of readers and what he dislikes excites their disapproval, his discourse may become a major item in the literature I have labelled normative doctrine.

In discussing descriptions of single entities earlier in this essay, I stated that many studies limit the descriptive account to whatever seems needed to support an analysis or critique which the author intends to make. Many descriptions of value-laden situations are subordinated to analysis and critique of the value positions revealed in the events which occurred. Some of the items to be cited immediately fall in this category. But the list of citations includes also writings in which the effort to describe predominates and criticism of what took place is limited. Regardless of how the descriptions are designed and regardless of the emphasis placed on value implications, all of these studies seem to me noteworthy in appraising our contributions to normative doctrine. References are: Four books by Denna F. Fleming, *The Treaty Veto of the American Senate* (Putnam's Sons, 1930), *The United States and the League of Nations* (Putnam's Sons, 1932), *The United States and World Organization, 1920–1933* (Columbia University, 1938), and *The United States and the World Court* (Doubleday Doran, 1945); Kenneth Colegrove, *The American Senate and World Peace* (Vanguard, 1944); Joseph Jones, *Fifteen Weeks* (Viking, 1955); H. H. Wilson, *Congress: Corruption and Compromise* (Rinehart, 1951); Lawrence H. Chamberlain, *Loyalty and Legislative Action: A Survey of Activity by the New York State Legislature, 1919–1949* (Cornell University, 1951); Robert K. Carr, *The House Committee on Un-American Activities, 1945–1950* (Cornell University, 1952); Mulford Q. Sibley and Philip E. Jacob, *Conscription of Conscience:*

The American State and the Conscientious Objector, 1940–1947 (Cornell University, 1952); Morton Grodzins, *Americans Betrayed; Politics and the Japanese Evacuation* (University of Chicago, 1949); and Jacobus ten Broek, Edward N. Barnhart, and Floyd W. Matson, *Prejudice, War and the Constitution* (University of California, 1954).

PROPOSALS FOR SOCIAL ACTION

Proposals for social action are not easily differentiated, in many cases, from normative doctrine. This, for two reasons. *First,* many items in our literature are obviously concerned with both. The author examines issues of value, impresses his value position on his discourse, and makes specific recommendations for maintaining existing social instruments, for altering them, or for replacing certain instruments with others he thinks more likely to advance us toward the ends he has endorsed. Several of the writings listed above as contributions to normative doctrine contain recommendations for revision of public policies and altering political institutions. *Second,* all social action has value implications. Any proposal to continue or change a policy, to preserve an institution intact or modify it, to abolish organizations and replace them with new structures—any such proposal grows out of value commitments and if made effective has impacts on value commitments. As proposals for social action rise on a scale of comprehensiveness, involving greater and greater complexes of interconnected arrangements and practices, the value implications are enlarged—i.e., increasing numbers of particular values are involved, or more generalized values, approaching what some call ultimate values, are involved.

Recognizing that normative doctrine and proposals for social action merge, it is nonetheless an easy matter to identify writings having as their major purpose the recommendation of social action that seems desirable to the author. In discussing normative doctrine, I cited authority for the view that American political scientists have produced little that boldly declares and carefully justifies the writer's value preferences. We suffer no like dearth of writings that boldly state the author's convictions about need for social action, whether it be maintenance of what we have or replacement of what we have with something else. Indeed, one often hears it said that a great preoccupation of American political scientists with social engineering is the principal explanation of why we produce far less than is generally thought desirable of both normative doctrine and exacting descriptive accounts.

The range of affairs embraced in our proposals for social action is indeed inclusive. It would not be greatly in error to say that every aspect of contemporary life which the American political scientist has studied he has sought to bolster up and sustain or sought to improve by recommendations for change. Professor Leonard D. White noted (No. 89 at pp. 15–16) some consequences of our social engineering in these words:

> It would be fruitless to follow political scientists into all their professional societies and all the "reform" groups through which they work. Suffice it to say that where good works are to be done on the body politic, there political scientists are to be found.

·   ·   ·   ·   ·

> Political scientists took a major responsibility for the reconstruction of municipal government, the hottest of our governmental problems in the first decade of the century. They led the way in the reorganization of state governments in the second and third decades. They were influential in the drive for a short ballot and better election procedures. They were chiefly responsible for educating the American public to the necessity of a budget system. They began the long process of discussion that finally, with the powerful help of circumstances, reversed the historical direction of American foreign policy.

Proposals for social action are made in many different types of writing. It would be difficult to find a textbook for any course dealing with government and politics in the United States that does not make a case for retention of or change in institutions, organizational structure, or practices; in many of them, endorsements of what exists and recommendations for improvements are featured. Studies that are primarily descriptive in nearly all cases indicate, usually in explicit language, the author's convictions about the best means for doing what we are trying to do; in many cases they recommend we quit doing what we are trying to do and set about doing something quite different. Articles in professional journals that report recent innovations in organizations or policies are pretty certain to provide evaluations that prophesy success or failure or imply need for further engineering in the matters under consideration. Not a few books on the shelves are prescriptive from start to finish, description of existing arrangements and practices and analysis of complicated and perplexing problems being distinctly subordinated. I make these statements with the literature relating to American government especially in mind. I am told that prescribing means for achieving ends approved by the author is equally prominent in our literature relating to international affairs.

Because preoccupation with social engineering so pervades our literature, it would be superfluous to offer an array of our efforts to influence social action. For the benefit of newcomers to the profession I cite a few items selected either because of the high prestige they have enjoyed among political scientists or because of the boldness with which social action of highest significance is urged. Three books which are addressed to a wide range of problems in American government and politics are: William Y. Elliott, *The Need for Constitutional Reform; A Program for National Security* (Whittlesey House, 1935); Arthur C. Millspaugh, *Democ-*

racy, Efficiency, Stability; An Appraisal of American Government (Brookings Institution, 1942); Arthur N. Holcombe, *Our More Perfect Union; From Eighteenth-Century Principles to Twentieth-Century Practice* (Harvard University, 1950). Dealing with the President, or Congress, or with relations between the two branches are: Woodrow Wilson, *Congressional Government* (Houghton Mifflin, 1885); Pendleton Herring, *Presidential Leadership* (Farrar and Rinehart, 1940); Caleb Perry Patterson, *Presidential Government in the United States* (University of North Carolina, 1947); James M. Burns, *Congress on Trial* (Harper, 1949); Joseph P. Harris, *The Advice and Consent of the Senate* (University of California, 1953); and American Political Science Association, Committee on Congress, *The Reorganization of Congress* (Public Affairs Press, 1945). On the American party system and problems of popular control of government are: James Allen Smith, *The Spirit of American Government* (Macmillan, 1907); Arnold B. Hall, *Popular Government* (Macmillan, 1921); E. E. Schattschneider, *Party Government* (Rinehart, 1942); American Political Science Association, Committee on Political Parties, *Toward a More Responsible Two-Party System* (Supplement to *American Political Science Review,* Vol. 45, No. 3, September, 1950); and Paul T. David, editor and author, *Presidential Nominating Politics in 1952* (5 vols.; Johns Hopkins, 1954). Urging reform in state government are: A. E. Buck, *The Reorganization of State Administration in the United States* (Columbia University, 1938), and American Political Science Association, Committee on American Legislatures, *American State Legislatures* (Crowell, 1954). The council-manager form of government is recommended for cities in Leonard D. White, *The City Manager* (University of Chicago, 1927), and in two volumes by Harold A. Stone, Don K. Price, and Kathryn H. Stone, *City Manager Government in Nine Cities,* and *City Manager Government in the United States* (both Public

Administration Service, 1940). Two books that have had great influence on theory and practice in administration are: Frederick A. Cleveland and A. E. Buck, *The Budget and Responsible Government* (Macmillan, 1920), and William F. Willoughby, *Principles of Public Administration* (Brookings Institution, 1927). For recommendations of policies, organization, or practices in respect to American foreign policy and international relations see the writings of Fleming and Colegrove cited above at p. 119; Charles A. Beard, *The Open Door at Home; A Trial Philosophy of National Interest* (Macmillan, 1934); and Hans Morgenthau, *In Defense of the National Interest* (Knopf, 1951).

part III

INTELLECTUAL CONFLICTS
WITHIN AMERICAN
POLITICAL SCIENCE

VII

Have We Tackled Too Much?

In the first chapter of this essay I suggested that four sources of doubt and fear account for the apprehension of those who are worried about the state of political science: (1) Fear that we engage too much in activities which divert us from scholarly study and adversely affect the quality of the studies we make; (2) Fear that we have set ourselves too great a task in scholarly study; that we have committed ourselves to objectives of inquiry which in magnitude and diversity are too great to be encompassed in a discipline; (3) Doubt that our scholarly enterprise promises to achieve results worthy of a place in the total structure of learned literature; (4) Doubt that we have fitted our efforts adequately with the efforts of other disciplines sharing with us the whole study of social relationships.

I have set forth already (in Chapter I) what seem to me main points of division and main contentions relating to the first of these four items. It remains to examine intellectual conflict stemming out of the other three sources of doubt and fear. The examination will necessarily be less than complete; I can only hope that I do not overlook issues of major importance and that I do not miss the main contentions likely to come out if all parties to controversy were allowed to enter briefs. I shall develop my analysis of the dispute about five questions: (1) Have we committed ourselves to an assignment of scholarly inquiry that is too inclusive for a single learned discipline? (2) If our present assignment is too inclusive, what should we make our principal foci of attention in a less comprehensive area of inquiry? (3) Does our writing reveal a sufficient compliance with the mood and mode of scientific inquiry? (4) What treatment should we give to matters we commonly call values? (5) At least partially subsumed under the preceding issues, but requiring special consideration because of the nature of current debate: What use shall we make of classic political writings in study and teaching?

The first of these questions is the subject matter of this chapter.

A BILL OF COMPLAINTS

If Part II of this essay is believed to provide a near-accurate account of what American political scientists have committed themselves to study, it must be admitted that our assignment is an enormous one. We appear determined to acquire a full understanding of legal government and our view of what constitutes full understanding is bold and inclusive, rather than conservative and restrictive. We are committed to description of governments in their many variations of form and process; to analysis of ideas about government; to construction of a science of politics; to development of normative doctrine; and to formulation and sponsorship of programs of social action.

There is widespread conviction among political scientists that this is too inclusive an assignment for a single discipline. This judgment rests on one or both of two grounds: (1) One may believe that a license to examine so much invites men to examine many things superficially, creates too little compulsion to examine anything definitively. (2) One may believe that the assignment is a commitment to incompatibles; that a group of scholars who are determined to do certain of these things as they should be done will of necessity be precluded from doing well some of the other things.

The evidence usually adduced to prove that we spread ourselves too thin and that superficiality prevails over profundity was in large part suggested in the preceding chapter. I noted that few of our descriptive accounts approach the quality exhibited in the model performances which demonstrate what we can do if we make imaginative and accurate description our goal. I reported that our literature that offers intensive analysis of ideas seems far from imposing when measured against the products of political scientists in other countries and students in other disciplines. I concluded that our efforts to construct a science are limited and that our contributions to normative doctrine usually are subordinated to another objective in our writing.

If one concede that our study tends to be superficial, he may still question whether this be due to the magnitude and diversity of our assignment or be due to some other conditioning circumstances. I do not recall having heard a persuasive statement of why one should think that the evidences of superficiality (such as they may be) are mainly due to the sweep of our undertaking. Three points, often heard, are worth mentioning however.

One, it is said that our concern with immediate education of the citizenry leads to scatteration of attention rather than concentration. Writing addressed to inclusive publics, to be effective communication, must be put in simple language, but the necessity for simple statement does not require that the analysis which precedes the write-up be partial or superficial. The reason such writing so often rests on partial or superficial analysis is this: we feel an obligation to advise publics on so many matters of current concern that we have not the manpower to make comprehensive and exacting inquiry before we lay the report before our audience.

Two, it is said that our determination to provide up-to-date descriptions of many if not all legal governments requires us repeatedly to do our work over. A revolution occurs in Europe and previous descriptions of a former government must be replaced by new descriptions of a new government. Congress and President enact some new legislation and the textbooks on American government must be rewritten.

Three, it is said that our visions of outer boundaries containing the discipline's subject matter foster impulses to account for, or make a place in our literature for, about everything that falls within those boundaries. Intensive examination of some things must wait, we seem to think, until we have identified and put on record about everything that comes within the limits of our area of concern. Not long ago, and quite likely today, a primary injunction to the candidate for the Ph.D. degree went like this: "Find out whether anyone has written on this subject; if anyone has, don't attempt a dissertation on that subject; if another person tackles your subject after you begin, either finish before him or be prepared to abandon your subject and start work on a new one." Replicative studies are almost unknown among American political scientists. Not only do we abhor replicative studies in which one man checks the findings of another man, we make few studies that lie side by side with another study and extend previous findings to additional areas of application. Lowell published his analysis of the influence of party on voting in American state legislatures in 1901. Some twenty-five years later we had studies by Stuart Rice which were fairly close to the pattern set by Lowell. Not until 1952 (a full half-century after Lowell) when William Keefe published his findings on the Illinois assembly (No. 110) did we put in print a study which relates Lowell's conclusions to other places or other times. The delay in extending Lowell's inquiry may not typify our practice but it is by no means an exceptional experience.

One who concludes we have tackled too much because he sees evidence that superficiality triumphs over thoroughness may listen to argument that we can retain the assignment and overcome the impulse to be superficial. One who believes our present assignment includes commitments that are incompatible with one another is less likely to be convinced that we can preserve the assignment and also greatly improve our scholarly product. While I have heard more than a few political scientists say that incompatibles are there, I am still not sure I understand what they believe to constitute incompatibility. It seems unlikely that any individual political scientist is restrained from doing scholarly work because one set of expectations or standards honored by the discipline commands him to tackle a problem or pursue a method which another set of norms brands as unworthy. It can hardly be meant that the determination of some political scientists to achieve certain objectives makes it impossible for other political scientists to achieve other objectives. It may, however, be argued with considerable force that the profession as a whole is unlikely to succeed in one or another great objective (e.g., construct a science of politics) if a major portion of the profession is busy at other objectives (e.g., describing legal governments in all their variations). It may be the case that individual political scientists who are heavily committed to development of normative doctrine by a speculative method are unavoidably inhibited from establishing effective means to given ends by a method which seeks proof for propositions in the empirical data of actual experience. It may also be the case that no single political science department can at any one time give oncoming political scientists adequate training for competent performance of all the pursuits that make up the whole scholarly enterprise to which the profession now stands committed.

The charge of superficiality, if sustained, does not require us to redefine the objectives or goals of our discipline. The charge of incompatibility, if sustained, does require reconsideration and redefinition. Both charges, that of invitation to superficiality and that of combination of incompatibles, may be answered by denying the evidence offered in support of the charge or by admitting proof of superficiality or incompatibility and denying that they are present in a degree sufficient to mar significantly the quality of our work. I have no doubt that most American political scientists stand behind one or the other of these two lines of defense.

But not all of us do. Certainly a substantial number of American political scientists are convinced that far too much of our literature is far too low in quality. What are the consequences of agreement on this? One man may deny that low quality (superficiality) is due mainly or even in any part to the sweep of the assignment; he may say it is caused by poor training of political scientists or because they are a bunch of inferior human beings or because of something else not inherent in the magnitude and diversity of the matters political scientists are committed to study. Another man may say that the scope of our assignment does invite superficiality; admit that we have responded to the invitation up to now; but yet insist that we can resist the invitation in the future. Neither of these men is required to reconsider the scope of our assignment with a view to reducing the range of matters we give attention to. For each of them the correction of our shortcomings lies somewhere else. For a third man this happy conclusion is not possible. He sees in our entire set of objectives a combination of incompatibles. Some things we are committed to do make it impossible to do some other things we are committed to do. Stated less drastically, an exemplary accomplishment of certain objectives requires the profession to so mobilize and direct its resources that it is rendered incapable of accomplishing certain other of its objectives in exemplary fashion. One who has such a belief has no alternative but to recommend that his profession make a choice among alternative sets of objectives, drop all but one set from its agenda, and thereafter concentrate attention on the set which is retained.

A PLEA IN AVOIDANCE

If the above reasoning is sound, it follows that there is not just one answer but many answers to the contention that American political scientists have undertaken to study too much and ought to cut down the scope of their assignment. I could not hope to think up the varying arguments which would represent views of persons standing in the several different positions indicated above. It will be sufficient, I think, to note the argument of some political scientists who contend that we ought not draw in the boundaries of our attention one bit, who contend that the virtues of political science spring mainly from the magnitude and diversity of the matters to which we give attention. At risk of greatly misunderstanding their position, I suggest that their argument runs as follows.

The study of human relationships suffers from overspecialization. Historians who concentrate on the distant past illuminate the problems which afflict man and man's experience in dealing with his problems, but some opportunities for fuller illumination are lost because the scholar who knows so much about long-past experience is not equally attentive to contemporary experience. The psychologist who approaches microscopic scrutiny of some aspects of man learns things we need to know, but the closeness with which he peers causes him to misinterpret much of what he sees and blinds him to still other important data within his field of vision.

The philosopher and the student of philosophy perform admirably in criticizing what is offered as knowledge, in bringing items of knowledge into syntheses, in establishing tests and constructing rational models that guide inquiry by others; but the literature produced by philosophers and students of philosophy suffers because too often the one who writes lacks contact with the empirical world he imaginatively describes or analyzes.

Similarly for the other social study disciplines; each greatly illuminates understanding of man but each suffers disabilities inherent in its focus of attention or method of observation and analysis.

A well-balanced battery of approaches to the study of human relationships makes a place for a discipline which focuses attention on a significant integrated area of affairs (a terrain) and resorts to every tested and tried method of inquiry in order to acquire a full understanding of that subject matter. Political science is so described. Legal government is the object of attention, the terrain; political scientists seek to learn everything significant about (acquire full understanding of) that object of attention; to get that knowledge they pursue every method of inquiry thought promising, appropriating them freely from other disciplines.

It is not suggested that political science, because it is characterized as just indicated, is superior to any other social study discipline. It is contended only (1) that a discipline so characterized usefully supplements the other existing disciplines, and (2) that more would be lost than gained to the whole study of human relationships if political scientists, in order to achieve a greater specialization, narrowed their object of attention, or sought to acquire less inclusive knowledge about the matters they study, or confined their inquiries within stricter methodological limits.

Men who are joined together in one discipline have essentially the same training, read most attentively a common
literature, and see much of one another in face-to-face con-
tacts. Stimulation to inquiry, sharing of ideas and experiences in planning inquiry, communication of results of
inquiry—all these take place most effectively within a single
discipline. Because they are united in the same discipline,
the political scientist who is mainly an analyst of ideas developed in previous literature influences the political scientist
who mainly describes what exists and occurs when the latter
makes his decisions about what to examine and what to look
for in the course of examination. Because they are united
in the same discipline, those political scientists who are
motivated to do social engineering acquire vision from those
political scientists who specialize in value theory and are
instructed in their design of means to ends by other political
scientists who specialize in scientific inquiry. And so on
through other relationships of special interests in objects of
attention, special concerns with kinds of knowledge, special
devotions to methods of inquiry. If it be said that this is a
view of a discipline that, for a limited universe of study, tries
to reproduce and combine the characteristics and qualities
of all other social study disciplines, admit it. Grant that
political science, in that case, cannot equal other disciplines
in utilization of their most highly developed skills; we may
hope to counterbalance that shortcoming by a fuller response
to the baffling fact that all reality is interrelated and separation of any part of it for close examination removes from
observation a part of what we are most concerned to understand.

CHAPTER VIII

Which Way Should We Turn?

Political scientists, like other people, are likely to tell their critics to be constructive, not just destructive. So members of our profession who say that the study of political science embraces too much feel an obligation to propose what the scope of inquiry should be cut down to. A number of different formulations have been submitted in recent years. Some of them have attempted a new identification of the objects of inquiry; i.e., they have proposed a terrain for exploration which has boundaries significantly different from those suggested by the phrase legal government. Others have suggested that legal government may still provide the best subject matter for exploration, but have recommended that we seek different kinds of knowledge (ask different kinds of questions) about that subject matter. Still other members of the profession, dissatisfied with the performance of American political scientists to date, believe our shortcomings lie mainly in our methods of inquiry and have urged a change of emphasis in general approaches to matters of interest and in means adopted for obtaining and analyzing data.

So far no one has sold his formula to the profession as a whole. No matter what is recommended, substantial numbers of political scientists offer reasons for believing it is better to go on as we have in the past than to make the proposed change. The remainder of this essay examines controversy which turns on dissatisfaction with what we are now doing and proposals for redirecting our efforts. In the paragraphs immediately following we give attention to two widely discussed formulations of the central object of inquiry (terrain) most likely to prove fruitful for political scientists: David Easton's "authoritative allocation of values for a society" and the variously worded notion of "power," "influence," or "power and influence." These two cases are noted because they disclose the kind of controversy that ensues when anyone proposes to redirect the attention and activities of political scientists. It must not be supposed that these are the only proposals for a reorientation of political scientists which strike me as interesting or significant.

AUTHORITATIVE ALLOCATION OF VALUES FOR A SOCIETY

In *The Political System* (Knopf, 1953) David Easton counseled us that political science ought to be conceived as the study of authoritative allocation of values for a society. I do not suggest that Easton thought the assignment he specified would be less inclusive than the one I view as our present commitment—full understanding of legal governments; it may be that Easton believed his formulation adds more to what we have traditionally studied than it takes away. Easton's mission, if I understand him correctly, was not to mark out new boundaries for political scientists. His central purpose was to set forth his judgment as to why the literature we have produced to date does not have higher social significance than it does and as to what new resolves and changes in procedure promise to yield improvement in our literature. He did not write a book to tell us that our inquiry will become more significant if we conceive our area of concern to be "authoritative allocation of values for a society."

He wrote a book to examine the conditions of fruitful inquiry, and in order to help political scientists appreciate how they can realize those conditions, he stated what he thinks ought to be the area of concern shared by political scientists. So I understand the book. (See No. 104 for an extended critique of Easton's book.)

Whatever be the facts about Easton's intentions, his formulation of the central object of inquiry, the area of concern or terrain of political science, attracted most interested attention among political scientists and became the point of considerable argument. Some political scientists find Easton's position unclear, saying they do not understand what he meant to identify in his statement that political science is the study of "authoritative allocation of values for a society." Others who think they understand him differ as to whether Easton only offers a new statement of just what political science has been for a considerable time, the study of legal governments, or whether Easton proposes an extension of the area of attention to matters not previously counted within the assignment of political scientists.

Doubt as to what Easton proposes seems to center on the words "authoritative" and "values." Easton asserts that values can be allocated authoritatively by means other than governmental decision or legal pronouncement; political science therefore attends to more than legal government. He states that "a policy is clearly authoritative when the feeling prevails that it must or ought to be obeyed," provided, I understand, that the feeling of obligation is sufficient to induce widespread compliance with the policy. Common behavior which is common because people feel they ought to behave that way is therefore authoritatively prescribed behavior. One is forced to ask: Is there any common behavior which is not authoritatively prescribed? What reason do people have for acting the same way, except that they share a feeling that they ought to act in that way? A common practice of scratching the head when it itches may be purely coincidental behavior not induced by a feeling that others expect one to scratch and therefore that one had better scratch. But a common practice of not interrupting preachers in church is induced by suppositions as to what others expect. Biologically stimulated actions like scratching the head appear not to be authoritatively prescribed; but common practices which are collective responses to the expectations of other people, like maintaining silence during sermons, do appear to be authoritatively prescribed. Surely under this reasoning every common behavior pattern which any social scientist would count significant becomes an authoritative prescription.

If the reasoning is sound to this point, Easton would have the political scientist study all socially significant common behavior patterns which allocate values. Our society has authoritatively determined—proven by common behavior in response to common expectations—that we will make great noise at sporting events, but be relatively quiet during services in church; that the dress of men will approach uniformity, but the dress of women will show far greater variety; that laboring men will frequently bargain for wages and other terms of employment through labor unions, but owners and managers of business firms will bargain ordinarily as individual firms and not through associations of firms. In Easton's formulation, all such determinations are the subject matter of political science, unless it be concluded that the matters which are affected by these determinations are not values.

I am aware that many a good argument has been lost because of a poor illustration. It may be that my examples of noise and silence, conformity and variance in dress, and organization for bargaining about terms of employment will appear to some readers not to involve values, or if they involve values, the values are not allocated by authority, or if such values are authoritatively allocated, they are not allocated for the whole of a society. If so, let them substitute their own examples of determinations which seem to meet the three tests and which are not allocated by authority of legal government.

A reading of Easton's entire book supports a conclusion that he would not have political scientists extend their inquiry to all determinations of the kind referred to above, but he is certainly less than clear as to why he would remove some or all of those matters from their attention. Are those matters (my examples or yours) not values in Easton's view, or are the determinations not authoritative? If you conclude (1) that any of those matters do not involve values, you reach that conclusion without help from Easton's language. But you are left to wonder what types, levels, or orders of things desired or approved of are values in Easton's view. If you conclude (2) that Easton regards those matters as values but denies that the common patterns of behavior are authoritatively determined, you hold that Easton did not really mean to say that a determination is authoritative "when feeling prevails that it ought to be obeyed."

If Easton does not stand by his assertion that "a policy is clearly authoritative when the feeling prevails that it must or ought to be obeyed," you have little choice but to conclude that he views only pronouncements of legal governments as authoritative for the whole of a society and therefore sees legal governments as the central object of inquiry for political science. That conclusion is induced by this line of reasoning. There seem to be just two ways of stating where authoritativeness lies. One, you can observe what people do, say that arrival at a common position is proof that an authoritative determination was made, and assert further that the process by which the many (regardless of individual motivations or rationales) came to a common position gave the determination whatever authoritativeness it had. Or two, you can say authoritativeness is fixed by a previous determination of society that a particular source of subsequent determinations will carry more "oughtness to obey" than all other sources.

What particular sources of decisions and expressions can you find that might outweigh in authoritativeness a generalized or amorphous source like the process by which a population arrives at a practice of yelling at ball games and maintaining silence during sermons? Religious systems and legal governments seem most likely candidates. A reading of Easton's entire book discourages a conclusion that he would have political scientists examine the processes of decision-making, instruction, and sanction manifested by religious organizations. So you conclude the study of authoritative allocation of values for a society must mean the study of what legal governments do, and that in turn means that the proper enterprise of political scientists is only a more intelligent and more diligent doing of just what they have long been doing.

The extraordinarily high praise which Easton's *The Political System* has received makes it clear that a very great number of political scientists find his formulation—political science is the study of authoritative allocation of values for a society—readily understandable, convincing, and satisfying. The preceding paragraphs attempt to make equally clear why some other political scientists (1) are uncertain as to what he proposes, or (2) conclude that he would push political science into a range of subject matter that is task enough for all the social sciences, or (3) conclude that he would leave political science just what it has been—the study of legal governments including the near-equivalents of legal government where legal government has not appeared.

POWER

Perhaps the most widely endorsed recommendations for a new focus of attention by political scientists would make the study of power our primary object of concern. Proposals which have been offered vary in verbal statement, and appear to vary substantially in intent. One of the earlier statements which received serious consideration by American political scientists was that of George E. G. Catlin, who said in his *The Science and Method of Politics* (Knopf, 1927, at pp. 205 and pp. 210–11) that "man in his relation to the wills of his fellows in control, submission and accommodation . . . is the characteristic of the 'political situation' "; and that "Politics, as a theoretical study, is concerned with the relations of men, in association and competition, submission and control, in so far as they seek, not the production and consumption of some article, but to have their way with their fellows." A later identification of the field of political science in different words seems not intended to modify the position Catlin announced in the book. (See No. 103 at p. 8.)

Harold Lasswell, in one of his earlier books, *Politics: Who Gets What, When, How?* (Whittlesey House, 1936, at p. 3 and elsewhere) stated that "the study of politics is the study of influence and the influential." In a later book of which he shared the authorship with Abraham Kaplan, *Power and Society* (Yale University, 1950, at p. xii), Lasswell said, "We conceive of political science as one of the policy sciences— that which studies influence and power as instruments of such integration [i.e., the integration of values realized by and embodied in interpersonal relations]." In the paragraph following, this statement is referred to as a "definition of political science."

Other formulations by other writers can be found which make influence, or power, or influence and power the primary or the sole object of concern for political scientists. For convenience of expression, I shall refer to the study which they recommend as the study of power.

It may be that virtually all writing by political scientists can be shown to have some bearing on a collective effort to understand the nature, manifestations, and consequences of power. It may also be the case that recent and contemporary writing shows more concern than earlier writing to get directly to significant aspects of power. Whatever the fact may be on these points, it seems an unavoidable conclusion that American political scientists have not generally accepted and acted upon the advice given by Catlin and Lasswell. Contemporary study by American political scientists is not addressed to power as forthrightly as Catlin, Lasswell, and some others have recommended.

Someone who was no doubt wise as well as witty wrote that Christianity was not tried and found wanting; rather, he said, it was found wanting and not tried. It may be that most political scientists who shy away from power as the central concern of political science have found it wanting before giving it a trial; I am certain that many of them took their adverse position without having made a careful effort to ascertain and appraise the implications of what was proposed. I have read only three extended efforts to examine and evaluate the Catlin and Lasswell proposals, one by William Y. Elliott on Catlin (No. 5 at p. 70), an article by David Easton on Lasswell (No. 69), and the section in Easton's book (pp. 115–24) on both Catlin and Lasswell. Elliott rejects Catlin and Easton rejects both Catlin and Lasswell. The grounds on which the two rejections stand are essentially the same, and they seem to me inappropriate to the discourse.

Elliott says (p. 84) that political science can "hardly achieve simplification unless it focuses its study on associational activities where they become governmental. Group discipline, say of the church, the trade-union, or the professional association, partakes of the nature of government and is 'political' in the broadest sense of that term. It becomes of interest to political scientists, however, only by way of comparison; or when it affects rights and duties general to citizenship; or when it infringes upon the sphere of other groups. Mr. Catlin's definition in this respect seems to be merely sociology with economics dubiously left out."

Easton says (at p. 123 of his book), "Both writers [Catlin and Lasswell] argue that all power relations, wherever they may exist, are automatically an index of the presence of a political situation. For these writers the hierarchical arrangement of relationships within a criminal band or in a respectable fraternal club both testify to the existence of political life there. The realization of this implication when politics is described as power, pure and simple, reveals the excessive breadth of the definition. Not that Catlin and Lasswell were wrong in maintaining that political science is and ought to be interested in these phenomena, but they were misleading when they failed to point out that political scientists are not concerned with them for their own sake. The definition is too broad, for political science is not interested in the power relations of a gang or a family or church groups simply because in them one man or group controls the actions of another. It might be necessary, to be sure, to devote time to such a comprehensive examination of power situations in order to develop a generalized theory of power. This theory would be very helpful to the political scientist, but by the nature of his task he directs his attention not to power in general but to political power. What Catlin and Lasswell, and in fact many power theorists, neglect to clarify is the distinction between power in general and power in a political context."

These answers are appropriate if one reads Catlin and Lasswell as having said: "Power as I have identified it is what political scientists have been and are studying. Political scientists understand political science to be the study of power as I have identified power." I do not understand Catlin and Lasswell to intend to make any such statements. I understand them to intend to be understood this way: "In order for a scientific study to emerge, stemming out of the past and present study carried on by political scientists, political scientists ought to (must?) redirect their attention, focusing on power as I have identified power." An argument that an act of domination which occurs in the Catholic church ought to be identified as and labelled a political act is not answered by the statement that such an act has not heretofore been and is not now generally identified and labelled a political act. An argument that political scientists ought to shift to a new central object of study is not answered by the statement that the proposed object has not been and is not now the central object of their study.

The proposals of Catlin and Lasswell are not identical. Lasswell's concept of influence appears to include all that Catlin meant to identify in control, submission, and accommodation, and a great deal more. If I understand correctly Lasswell's use of the term, influence can be observed or inferred when any man moves into a position more favorable for satisfying any of his wants vis-à-vis other persons; influence is manifested (in my favor) if, because I was wounded in battle, my companions hold doors open for me to walk through or a possible competitor refuses to bid for purchase of a house and lot I have indicated I would like to buy. I suspect that Catlin would say these occurrences are too far out on the margins of control, submission, and accommodation to be relevant and significant for political science. In any event, he explicitly excludes from the proper concern of political scientists decisions made in the market place as economists identify the market place. I presume he would also remove from our concern commercial advertising designed to condition behavior in the market place. In so doing he appears to have eschewed symmetry in fixing new boundaries for political science. One might have preferred a statement that political science embraces acts of control, submission, and accommodation wherever they occur, even in the production and consumption of articles, with an optimistic premise that political scientists would find much of their work being done for them by economists. Catlin did not say it that way.

There are two ways of looking at the charge Catlin and Lasswell give us. The first supposes they intended to identify a terrain, an area of human events which political scientists should explore throughout, describing all configurations that rise sufficiently in their consciousness to appear significant. Viewed as terrain, the Catlin-Lasswell formulation requires political scientists to examine all comings together, whether institutionalized or not, in which one human being exerts power (or power and influence) over another. The second way of looking at the recommendation of Catlin and Lasswell sees it not as defining an area or terrain to be explored but rather as identifying a kind of knowledge to be sought. Read this way, Catlin and Lasswell do not tell political scientists where to look but only what to look for. They do not say, find out and report everything of significance which falls within these boundaries of human affairs; rather they say, get interested in this type or style of human relationship, examine it wherever you can readily get at it, pursue the study wherever there is promise of getting the knowledge you seek without bar or discouragement because of institutional or other bounds heretofore thought to be limits for political scientists.

I think it probable that many political scientists have objected to a reorientation which makes power the principal object of their study because they have supposed the job of their discipline is to explore and describe what is found in an area of affairs, a terrain with recognizable boundaries. If one starts with this presumption, he will want to know in advance of his exploration what the boundaries are. He will want to know that the enclosure is sufficiently restricted to permit hope that the main features of the whole territory can be determined before the first explorations are rendered obsolete by changes that have taken place. He will shy away from an assignment which sets boundaries that also enclose all the other social sciences. Any political scientist who views the proposal to study power as a charge to examine all significant manifestations of influence might well be horrified by the sweep of the assignment indicated. Surely the whole exploration of relationships which can be hooked up to influence is too much for a single discipline in a group of social science disciplines. Are there any relationships among human beings that any social scientist would want to understand that do not fall under the heading of influence, as Lasswell defines influence? Surely, if there is to be a division of labor among several social science disciplines, and political science is to be co-ordinate with the others, the assignment to the political scientists of an area for exploration must include less than all that is embraced in influence. The same must be said for Catlin's recommendation if it is viewed as an injunction to scrutinize, describe, explain, and evaluate all significant institutions, situations, and events that manifest relationships of control, submission, and accommodation. Surely that terrain, while undoubtedly much less extensive than that proposed by Lasswell, is still far too extensive for one discipline that is companion to other social science disciplines.

The proposal that we study power may appear much less forbidding if it is viewed not as a charge to explore and report all significant manifestations of men influencing or exerting control over other men but rather as an admonition to examine certain kinds of relationships, observing them where significant manifestations are most readily found and limiting the inquiry to what advances understanding of the fundamental nature of the relationships. Let us suppose (without contending that either of them so intended) that Catlin and Lasswell are to be read as follows: "Political scientists have up to now set limits for their study which inhibit the search for understanding that any society badly needs. Forget these hitherto boundaries; identify problems—complexes of human relationships—which the training and experience of present-day political scientists fit them to study. Pursue the study of those problems without concern for previously recognized boundaries for study. Let experience in that study determine whether people who are in a line of descent from present-day political scientists find a particular problem-area they will identify and hold on to as a domain to be called political science. Or let experience in that study develop convictions that further fruitful study will best be carried on by several distinct disciplines, no one of which conforms to any of the social science disciplines we now recognize."

This interpretation of the challenge to study power may remove one cause for hesitancy—a conviction that it requires us to explore too much territory; it certainly stirs up two other objections.

First, it suggests that it is not important to preserve political science as a discipline having the essential character we have known up to now. On this interpretation of the proposal, we are not advised to abandon our present knowledge and skills or to turn present knowledge and skills to wholly new purposes. But we are advised to quit doing many things we are now doing, to heap up effort on some things we are already doing, and to turn our attention to many matters we have hitherto ignored. Such a reorientation in study must necessarily create unexpected needs in the training of entrants to the profession. Innovations in training will supply new visions of goals to be achieved. And so, we are warned, a later generation of scholars will have turned its back on much of our present-day scholarly enterprise, and what we now recognize as political science will have been replaced by a new discipline regardless of the name applied to the new activities. Undoubtedly there is, among American political scientists, a great loyalty to a tradition of which we are present-day custodians and to which, if the tradition continues, we contribute a link in a chain. Undoubtedly with many American political scientists this loyalty is so great that even a slight prospect of terminating that tradition or drastically altering its character will not be entertained. Things I have heard them say cause me to suppose that many members of the profession see in the proposal to make power our central object of inquiry a scheme to terminate a great tradition in scholarship and they oppose it for that reason.

Second, the proposal to make power our central object of inquiry has been challenged if not rejected by some political scientists who welcomed the suggestion and gave it thoughtful consideration. They find troublesome obstacles, if not insurmountable barriers, to meaningful study of power—obstacles in definition of the central concept, in identification of power manifestations, in differentiation of stimuli and responses, and in measurement of impact and response. I believe that we do not yet have in print a searching examination of the problems which the skeptic thinks certain to be encountered if power becomes our primary focus of attention. In addition to the difficulties acknowledged by Lasswell and Kaplan in their book, *Power and Society,* one gets some hints as to what obstacles may be ahead in a rapidly growing list of articles by American political scientists and other scholars. Some of the more probing items are: Agger (No. 100), Dahl (Nos. 14 and 105), Kaufman and Jones (No. 93), March (No. 40), Bierstedt (No. 102), Porter (No. 120), Schermerhorn (No. 124), and Simon (No. 85).

No doubt a broad front attack on the phenomena of power would involve daring forays of imaginative speculation as well as rigorous scrutiny of precise empirical data. It is a fact, however, that most writing about strategy for a study of power supposes a main reliance on diligent probing into the world of experience. Our consideration of the recommendation that political scientists make power rather than a full understanding of legal governments their primary concern is continued therefore in the next several paragraphs dealing with the dispute about the need to make political science more scientific than it is at present.

CHAPTER IX

How Scientific?

A substantial part of the intellectual conflict which plagues American political scientists is rooted in issues that are methodological in character. We part company on issues of methodology as methodology. And differences in position on a methodological issue reinforce differences in position on other matters, such as the proposal that power ought to be the central object of our study.

The issues of methodology that stir American political scientists most deeply, it seems to me, are related to the scientific character of our study. Do we apply the method of science when we study matters for which scientific method is appropriate? When we attempt to be scientific, do we actually meet minimum standards or tests of scientific method? Ought we limit our studies to matters that lend themselves to scientific inquiry, leaving to others the examination of whatever matters may not be appropriate for a scientific approach? For most recent evidence of conflict relating to these matters, see the article by James Prothro (No. 82) and the symposium of David Smith, David Apter, and Arnold Rogow (Nos. 55, 10, and 51).

Those who urge a fuller compliance with the mood and

mode of science cite one or more of three critical needs. They call for a resort, on a profession-wide basis, to scientific method (1) in order to improve the quality of our descriptive accounts, (2) in order to contribute to a unified social science, and (3) in order to determine effective means for achieving specified ends.

IMPROVEMENT OF DESCRIPTIVE ACCOUNTS

The case for closer compliance with the tests of science in descriptive study need not be elaborated. The examination of our descriptive literature in the preceding chapter sufficiently indicates why there is dissatisfaction with current attempts to describe. The key to more comprehensive and more accurate description is a resort to the methods of science. I am not aware that this is disputed among political scientists. I think all thoughtful political scientists acknowledge that descriptive statements ought to reach out according to tests of relevancy and probe inward according to tests of accuracy. Equally, I think they acknowledge that commitment to scientific method is a commitment to comprehensive and accurate description.

But there is fear that political scientists may become over-committed to scientific method. Scientific inquiry is characterized by mood as well as mode. And the mood has among its components a high exaltation of proof, a conviction that observed experience (empirical data) is supreme evidence, and a discontent with theories until they have been found to hold up when checked against observable experience (empirical referents). Indulgence in the mood of science has limited what the natural scientists inquire into. They do not grapple with the question: What must God intend for atoms to do in view of His determination to have good ultimately triumph over evil? And they do not grapple with a lot of other questions which are untinged by religious or magical implications and which have high social importance.

Many political scientists express a fear that an increase in attachment to scientific endeavor will be accompanied by elimination of significant questions from the profession's area of concern. The reasoning may be as follows. Scientific method is fine for inquiries that lend themselves to precise observation, measurement, quantitative analysis. But enchantment with the precision of science may cause political scientists to limit their inquiries to just what lends itself to precise empirical analysis. If so, certain kinds of inquiry which to date have proved highly fruitful, perhaps even our most fruitful, will drop out of our literature. The gains expected to accrue from utilization of scientific method where proper are not sufficient to justify assuming the risk that other types of inquiry will be driven out of our professional enterprise. Therefore, political scientists will be wise to move cautiously and with reservations in the direction of scientific endeavor; and it will be better to stay right where we are in methods of study if the alternative is to encourage anything like a stampede toward the method of science.

Two kinds of study are frequently cited as most likely to be depressed or terminated if the profession reveals a notable determination to become scientific. *One,* inquiry into value —especially efforts to determine the content of values and value systems, to clarify alternatives in choice among values, and to justify choice of certain alternatives over others. *Two,* formulation and exploration of the grand hypothesis. I have heard it said that the spirit of science is inimical to studies of the kind Weber made when he inquired into the relation of the Protestant ethic to capitalism, to studies of the kind Mill made when he sought to find what means of representation would both improve the quality of the population and enable government to be carried on effectively, to the argument and counterargument put forth by Hayek in *The Road to Serfdom* and those who rose to reject or affirm Hayek's position.

Controversy within the profession relating to study of values is discussed in the next chapter of this essay and therefore need not be further mentioned here. Concerning the grand hypothesis, I understand the pro-science wing of the profession would deny that anyone treasures the grand hypothesis more than the devotee of science. They cite the magnificent imaginative feats of Copernicus, Newton, Einstein, Darwin, and others as proof that science depends upon, produces, and explores constructs of imagination which run as far beyond ascertained fact as any hypothesis yet formulated and meaningfully explored in the literature of politics. Not only does science produce and explore grand hypotheses, say the defenders of science; the method of science is the best guarantor that knowledge will advance to that next stage which makes apparent the need for a more inclusive hypothesis and provides a base from which to launch the flight of imagination that produces the next hypothesis. Hans Reichenbach offers this assurance in *The Rise of Scientific Philosophy* (University of California, 1954, at p. 190): "Speculative philosophy has never exhibited a power of imagination equal to the ingenuity which scientific philosophy has displayed under the guidance of scientific experiments and mathematical analysis."

It seems to me these few remarks indicate the nature of disagreement within the profession about the need for fuller resort to science in order to improve the quality of our descriptive accounts. I doubt that anything I can say would remove any doubts, modify any convictions, alter any stances adopted for combat. The further comment on science and values which follows under other heads may help some of the newcomers to the profession move toward their own positions.

CONTRIBUTION TO A UNIFIED SOCIAL SCIENCE

The case for directing our efforts toward the construction of a unified social science rests on an analogy provided by the method and structure of knowledge commonly called the natural sciences. It presumes that there are regularities in the behavior of human beings, observable in the present, which will persist in the future. If we apply the natural science analogue to human relationships, our study is guided by a presumption that we can identify and describe some orderly relationships (patterns of occurrences) whose existence is not confined to the moment of first discovery but persists and may be verified at later times when careful efforts to observe are carried out.

If one is committed to the idea of cause and effect he may wish to call the regularities (presuming they exist) compulsions. In that case the presumption may be restated as follows: Human behavior is governed by compulsions which men cannot wholly avoid or alter, and which give direction to and set limits for their behavior; and further, the nature and effects of these supposed compulsions can be ascertained with sufficient accuracy to establish knowledge useful for guiding men in deciding upon action in areas where choice is available to them.

Anyone who is acquainted with the voluminous literature relating to cause and effect will acknowledge that this is no place to inquire whether the presumption of a cause-effect relationship in human behavior will prove helpful in study; whether, if presumed, the relationship can actually be proved; whether persistence of regularities in relationships over a long period of observation is sufficient ground for predicting existence of those regularities in the future, or whether, in order to predict, one must also presuppose that the regularities which have been observed are due to a cause-effect relationship; and so on. Because I wish the analysis which follows to be of equal value to people with different views, I shall use the terms regularity and compulsion interchangeably and without implication for or against the cause-effect relationship.

It should also be noted at this point that it makes no difference whether the presumed regularities or compulsions are thought to be biologically imposed or to be the product of culture. The questions significant for science are these: Can regularities actually be found, identified, observed? If some are found, can they be elaborately described? If found and described, can they be fitted together in significant, meaningful relationships?

The aspirations of those who seek to establish a unified social science are best appreciated when examined against a background of achievement in the natural sciences. Some further comment on experience in the natural sciences will accordingly be made even though this involves repetition of some things said earlier about construction of a science.

The goal of the scientist who deals with natural phenomena is to move as directly and as rapidly as possible to basic knowledge. Knowledge is basic as it supports an increasing structure of other knowledge. Stated another way, the scientist seeks to establish the broadest generalizations attainable, the breadth of any generalization being dependent on the range of phenomena to which it applies. When the generalized statement has been made, it is not only a summation of the findings out of which it was formulated; it suggests an explanation for previously baffling phenomena and guides further research. Experience in wave theory illustrates. Early generalizations about wave movements in water suggested that sound and light might also be transmitted by waves comparable to those in water. Subsequent refinements and elaborations of wave theory are now applied in study of subatomic relationships, even by investigators who are currently of the opinion that those relationships are not sufficiently like what has heretofore been called wave movement to justify prediction that they will ultimately be found to demonstrate the properties or characteristics of waves.

The first grounds for objection to a unified social science which one encounters among political scientists rest on a denial of the analogy to the natural sciences. It is said (1) that there are no regularities in human behavior (no compulsions which direct and limit human behavior) comparable to the presumed uniformity of nature; or (2) that if such regularities or compulsions exist they are not significant for understanding relationships among men; or (3) if they exist and are significant, we do not have the capacity or facilities for scrutiny which would yield sure identifications and dependable descriptions. Perhaps most people who stand in any of these positions find all three of them ground for rejecting the natural science analogy. I take it there is no way of learning which side is right on this issue except by making the search for regularities and either finding some which gain general acceptance or, failing to find them, there is general agreement that further search is futile. In any case, the literature on this issue is sufficiently familiar to make further comment here unnecessary.

Those who are willing to presume that significant regularities in human behavior do exist and may be found fall into dispute about how to start the search. How did the forerunners of contemporary natural scientists know that the examination of waves would pay off better than an equal expenditure of time and effort on examination of the movements of clouds or the movements of falling leaves? How did the early explorers know that a charting of the movements of heavenly bodies would pay off better than a charting of the movements of pebbles in flowing streams, or of birds flitting about from perch to perch? How can modern students of social relationships know whether an advance to broadest generalizations about human behavior is most likely to result from study of manifestations of influence, or from study of how judges justify their decisions, or from study that finds out who goes to the polls on election day and who stays away?

The answer to these questions appears to be that, at any stage of study and accumulation of knowledge, no one knows what further lines of inquiry will pay off in most direct and rapid advance to further generalizations that will win general acceptance. The first students of waves in fluids did not know that their findings would enter into an enduring structure of knowledge; in fact, many of the then most respected of their contemporaries made studies of other things now considered abortive if indeed anyone now knows what studies they made. But the successes and failures of men in the line of descent which gives us the natural scientist of our own times suggest at least two prime guides for making guesses.

First, your present state of knowledge, even if this be knowledge so elementary that it is shared by all observant people, makes you aware of certain regularities in the real world about you, and regularity suggests there must be reason for it which is worth understanding. Waves move in water in stable patterns; there must be something back of the visible movement worth knowing about if you can find it. There is a regularity also in falling leaves (they tend to move toward the earth), and study of falling bodies was another line of investigation started early which also paid off; but the study of directions taken by leaves propelled by wind did not pay off, if anyone undertook such study.

Second, the universality of phenomena also provides a guide in study which seeks to arrive at generalizations. If at a time when systematic study was emerging, one knew of only a single geyser in existence, it might be regarded as a plaything of the gods; to know how the gods made it work might explain little or nothing about that part of nature which served or oppressed man and which man wanted to learn how to conquer or avoid. Tendency to fall toward the earth was so general among different kinds of objects as to suggest that here is something which, studied in respect to one object, may provide understanding applicable to objects in general.

No doubt there are other useful guides for selecting points at which to start study of human behavior with maximum hope of arriving at generalizations, but these two will suffice for the analysis which follows. This analysis will be developed about study of influence as a special case. By confining our attention to one object of study, in this case influence, we should be able to get to the heart of current dispute about methodology and at the same time avoid the confusion that might result if we tried to relate the analysis to several possible objects of inquiry. We might have taken as our case interpersonal relations as posed in recent literature of sociology, or group and transaction as posed by Bentley, or the less precisely defined focus of attention currently labelled political behavior. I have chosen influence, rather than any of these other alternatives, in part because all who read this essay can be expected to agree that manifestations of influence are bound to be of high concern to political scientists no matter what turns our study may take, and in part because general familiarity with Lasswell's writings makes it possible to relate the analysis to his proposals for study of influence with a minimum of diversion for explanation of terms or concepts.

Influence, as an object of study, meets the two tests suggested above as guides in selecting subject matter for scientific exploration—universality of occurrence and manifestations of regularities. All can agree that influence occurs nearly always, if not always, when men come into contact with one another regardless of their purpose in coming together or other characteristics of the association; thus it meets the test of universality. Equally, all can agree that preliminary scrutiny reveals regularities in manifestations of influence; for instance, some persons appear regularly to bow down to certain other persons.

If the study of influence offers high hope of arriving at generalizations, why isn't the traditional study of political scientists right down the line? Legal governments are great systems of influence; they provide readily accessible demonstrations of power, which is influence backed up by compelling sanctions. The answer to this question is that legal governments do provide a good place to start studying influence, as Catlin and Lasswell pointed out, reiterated, and emphasized. The question which excites dispute is this: Do the kinds of studies political scientists have in the main been making provide information that seems likely to advance us rapidly and surely toward generalizations about regularities in human behavior or compulsions that direct and limit behavior? Those persons who deny that significant regularities exist or who assert that they are beyond our powers of detection are not party to this dispute; they have ruled themselves out by rejection of the presumptions which make the issue possible.

Among those who have counted themselves in on the dispute, the argument, it seems to me, runs like this.

1. Contention of Those Who Think Traditional Studies Inadequate

Those who are most convinced that traditional political science is inadequate nonetheless admit that it does provide knowledge helpful in getting ahead toward generalizations. But in their view traditional study, for purposes of establishing generalizations, has two shortcomings.

First, confinement of inquiry to legal governments reduces our chances of finding what we seek. It may be that legal governments provide all the manifestations of influence that need to be examined in order to arrive at broadest generalizations, but we do not know that. Men who study influence should feel free to carry the search to any point in the network of human relationships where they suspect the evidence they need can most readily be found. This point is not countered by saying that political scientists can make the study in legal governments and sociologists can make it in other institutions and places where man meets man.

Scholars must adjust themselves to a division of labor. But there is a loss of efficiency at the lines of junction. It is essential that individual scholars feel free to cross frontiers in hot pursuit of knowledge. Each scholar acquires knowledge which he cannot yet communicate to others. This knowledge is his personal equipment which he uses as he makes further studies. Other men, whether in his discipline or another, cannot tell him what he would find if he made the search in his way and with his equipment. He must do it himself.

The studies now predominating in political science do not carry the search for needed knowledge to great distances from what can be identified as legal government. Indeed, prevailing views about the subject matter of political science restrain men from carrying inquiry where they need to go. Teaching assignments do not reinforce research if research goes beyond legal governments. Doctoral dissertations which explore phenomena not closely related to legal governments are discouraged if not outlawed. Mature scholars who venture far from legal governments learn that they are no longer regarded by some of their peers as political scientists and have reason to fear that rise in social status and financial income will be retarded.

Second, for purposes of establishing generalizations about influence, traditional studies by political scientists are misdirected. Traditional fact-finding essays describe institutions and practices which are the embodiment of a vast number of choices. A unified social science cannot be constructed out

of findings which only report the product of a multitude
of choices. To contribute effectively to a unified social science, the findings must relate to how the choices were made;
more specifically, they must relate to the regularities or compulsions which direct and limit the choices. Only if we identify the regularities or compulsions can we begin to construct
a unified social science; if the presumed regularities or compulsions do not actually exist there will be no unified social
science.

It is true, the argument continues, that some political
scientists, completely within the tradition, do study the making of choices—the decision of a judge, the decision of an
executive or administrative official, the decision of a legislative assembly. Such studies may indeed advance the search
for generalizations about influence. But few if any of them
are probing enough. They tell you that the judge appeared
to move from a tentative position to his final position because of certain impacts on his mind. But what is identified
as making an impact is a package of items which need to be
separately identified and the force of each measured. The
search for regularities or compulsions requires us to reduce
to smallest items—the nearest approach we can make to elements—the things men attach value to; to find out how these
value items are put together in packs to cause other men
to maintain or alter behavior; to observe, and measure if
possible, the resistances of men (consciously or unconsciously
aroused) to packs of value items which are offered as inducements to maintain or alter behavior. The analogy provided
by the natural sciences teaches us that the broadest generalizations (basic knowledge which supports an increasing structure of other knowledge) are found as inquiry is pushed
further and further toward elements—smaller particles, sim-
pler relationships, most minute manifestations of movement.
A commitment to the construction of a unified social science
sets the scholar on just such a toilsome path.

2. Contention of Those Who Think Traditional Studies Are Adequate

In argument which rejects the reasoning just set forth and which justifies traditional political science literature as means of arriving at generalizations concerning influence, three points seem to me to stand out in cogency.

First, many if not most political scientists are firmly opposed to the first proposition made above in the case against traditional study. They believe that legal governments provide all the manifestations of influence that need to be examined in the course of constructing a science. They believe that properly designed studies of legal governments will disclose many regularities and support many generalizations applicable to influence in all manner of human associations. They believe further that traditional studies carry within themselves evidence of fixed determination to arrive at understanding of influence and of steady advance toward that goal. I think nothing more need be said here about this line of argument, since the truth on that point can only be learned by fuller exploration of influence connected with government and removed from government.

Second, it is argued that the training, previous research experience, and accumulated knowledge of present-day political scientists does not fit them to push exploration down to smallest items or elements. To advise political scientists to identify value items, find how they are cumulated into inducements, and measure resistances to inducements is to advise political scientists to abandon their expertise and find another expertise. It is advice to acquire expertise that probably can be supplied only to younger men who obtain their basic training in other disciplines. It is therefore advice to remove the next generation of political scientists from the political science department as a place to get their major instruction and training. The line of inquiry peculiar to a discipline ought not be terminated and its function in training young people ought not to be junked until it is established that what it is prepared to offer to society is too small in value to justify the cost of maintaining that discipline. The strongest proponents of a reorientation which would set political scientists on new types of search for generalizations about influence acknowledge that present study of political scientists is helpful to the inquiries they recommend. Beyond that, traditional political science supplies other highly useful contributions to knowledge. Conclusion: Let other disciplines take on the job of direct inquiry into the elementary conditions and manifestations of influence, or let a new discipline emerge to do that job; let the political scientists do what their training, experience, and existing capital investment fit them to do well.

Third, a point that sums up much of what was said in the first two. We never know what course of study will provide the most direct approach to dependable generalizations. Findings about the movements of heavenly bodies helped other men establish some of the properties of matter on earth, and findings in the physics laboratory contributed greatly to understanding of the composition and movements of heavenly bodies. The corpus of natural science includes the findings of inventors and engineers as well as the findings of men who declared their devotion to pure science. The kind of study now predominating among political scientists may someday be found to have contributed more to enduring generalizations than all the studies designed to pursue a more direct approach to generalizations.

The foregoing account, brief and partial as it is, will indicate the essential nature of intellectual conflict stemming out of the assertion that the prime objective of political science should be the construction of a unified social science. It seems unnecessary to extend the analysis, here applied to influence, to other central objects of study such as the concepts of group and transaction proposed by Bentley or the less precisely defined concepts which appear in a bundle called political behavior.

DETERMINATION OF EFFECTIVE MEANS
FOR ACHIEVING SPECIFIED ENDS

The third critical need for greater utilization of scientific method in political science has been labelled policy science. I think the gist of what is proposed under this label can be most accurately stated this way: A prime objective (or *the* prime objective?) of political scientists should be to determine the most effective means for achieving specified ends.

This is a charge which, no doubt, most political scientists can accept with enthusiasm. This is, in fact, what a great many of us have been trying to do. It may indeed be the case that virtually all our literature has a readily observable relationship to the search for effective means of achieving, through legal governments, a variety of ends which different societies or sectors of societies have fixed as goals. The great emphasis upon reform which characterizes so much of our literature is evidence of widespread concern to relate means to ends. Writing which appears to be sheer description of institutions or processes at least clears ground for later studies which proceed more directly to the establishment of means by which particular ends may be achieved. The most philosophic analysis of democratic ideals or of something called liberty or equality goes beyond the clarification and evaluation of recommended goals to tell us something about choices which must be made in order to achieve goals.

The proposal that we make the determination of effective means a prime objective of our study does not excite controversy within the profession. Controversy starts when statements are made about what constitutes suitable subjects of inquiry and about the best ways of carrying out investigations. It seems to me that dispute centers on these two points:

(1) need for a more direct attack on means-ends relationships, and (2) need for stricter compliance with scientific method.

1. Issue: Points of Attack

Proponents of a more rapid advance toward a policy science urge reconsideration of what political scientists select as subjects of study. Differences of opinion on this point will be sufficiently illustrated, I think, with study which attempts to provide descriptions.

The descriptive studies we have produced to date are found objectionable, not because their prime or sole purpose is to describe, but because of what they describe or because they do not carry description far enough. The most convincing statements we can make about means to ends are statements reporting what has been found to work as means in the real world. It has been said that science can do nothing but describe, and that explanation consists of elaborated description. Those who urge that we concentrate attention on means-ends relationships ask, above all, that we undertake descriptive studies, but they insist that we show better judgment in deciding what to study and that we carry our descriptions to the point where findings accumulate to become explanation.

Descriptive studies predominating in our literature are found inadequate by critics because those studies start a long way off and never get up to means-ends relationships. For an illustration which can offend no one more than the writer of this essay, take certain accounts of the composition of American state legislatures. Hyneman has recorded the means of livelihood of legislators, their ages, how far they went in school, how long they served before terminating legislative service, and some other characteristics, and has related these facts to the rural-urban character of the districts sending them to the legislature. But Hyneman has not presented a single statement, born out of his research, about the relation which any of these characteristics of legislators bears to any man's goal for performance by legislative bodies. He has shown that some American legislatures have much higher turnover in membership than some other legislatures, but he has not shown that short service or long service has an effect, favorable or adverse, on the quality of legislation enacted or on any other matter the legislature is supposed to attend to. Further, if you are willing to presume that longer service than now obtains would have a favorable effect on the quality of legislative performance, he has not provided any knowledge about how we can obtain longer legislative service. Hyneman, say the critics, should call a halt to his inventory of characteristics and at least try to ascertain the relationship between characteristics of legislators and legislative performance, if not to go beyond that to find out what can be done to create legislative institutions and select legislators who will behave in ways that please somebody better than present behavior.

The proposal that we make a more direct attack on means-ends relationships is not intended to force political science into narrow confines. We are invited to find out how to construct organizations so that they will give attention to this or that, proceed in this way or that, accomplish this or that goal with efficiency and economy; to find out how men can exert influence on government, and how government can exert influence on men; to find out how competing demands can be fitted into forceful governmental policy, and how governmental policies can be made effective instruments of social change. Inquiries strictly limited in scope and requiring elaborate analysis of precise data are desired. But direct attack on means to ends can also be made in studies which are most comprehensive in scope, which examine great packages of facts represented by historic and contemporary events, and which are most fruitfully examined by a speculative method.

Political scientists who on the whole are satisfied with the kind of descriptive studies we usually make have at least two main points on which to rest a reply to the foregoing argument.

First, on the point conceded by the critics—that traditional descriptive studies have some bearing on means-ends relationships—defenders of these studies say that their value for determination of effective means to specified ends is much greater than the critics admit. Most of our extended descriptions of institutions and the way things are done do more than describe what exists. They show the relationships among the parts that make up a whole, and in so doing they provide clues as to what will have to be done to make desired changes in the whole. Furthermore, what is described is not presented as something standing isolated; any good description of an institution or process places that institution or process in a bigger social context. And statements showing how it fits into a bigger social context are in large part observations about the effectiveness of the thing described as means to other ends.

Second, those who defend traditional descriptive studies point out that we write for a lay audience as well as a scholarly audience. A first requisite for intelligent participation in political life is familiarity with governmental institutions and political processes. This nation relies on the political scientist for much of the elementary information which is the foundation of an adequate citizen's understanding; the political scientist cannot fulfill his obligations to a democratic society if he supplies only a sophisticated analysis of means for achieving ends. The descriptions predominating in our literature are admirably suited to citizen needs. They point out to him the places where decisions are made, guide

him up the paths he must follow to stand in the presence
of authority, and tell him what he must do to convert his
wishes into influence on policy. Even the simplest descriptions of institutions and ways, therefore, equip the citizen
to make his own discoveries of effective means for achieving
ends, and at the same time provide the first steps toward
the more sophisticated analysis of means-ends relationships
which marks a distinguished literature of political science.

2. Issue: Adequacy of Method

That great part of our literature discussed earlier in this
essay under the heading of Proposals for Social Action meets
the test of direct attack on means-ends relationships. It is
condemned on the ground that too rarely do the evidence
and the analysis support the conclusions about what ought
to be done. The correction of the deficiencies, according to
many critics, lies in a stricter compliance with the mood and
mode of science.

There appear to be four main grounds of complaint against
our reform literature as means-ends analysis.

First, the ends for which means are sought are not sufficiently refined. Illustration: Responsible party government
is cited as an end to be achieved, and specific actions (recommended changes in institutions and practices) are offered as
means of achieving responsible party government. The term
responsible party government does not have an accepted
precise meaning in political science. Like Chesterton's cloth-
ing, which marked the spot where his body could be found,
this term only indicates an area of choice or range of alternatives. A prescribed change which, by general agreement,
may advance us toward something I call responsible party
government may inhibit something you call responsible party
government. For meaningful examination of possible means
to responsible party government the term must be given
an operational definition, i.e., reduced to something suffi-

ciently precise to permit no significant difference in interpretation. Thus, if the term is to be used in the analysis, responsible party government might be reduced to commitment of a majority of the party's members of the lawmaking assembly and the chief executive (if the party controls that office) to enactment of a program of legislation specified immediately prior to the last previous general election. If the end is stated in such precise terms, there can be hope of determining what may be effective means to the end, and readers of the analysis can evaluate the proposed means in the light of their own study and experience. Much of our reform literature, say its critics, does not state in such precise terms the end for which means is sought.

Second, much if not most of our reform literature fails to relate the end for which means are sought to other valued things not wholly compatible with this end. The end to be achieved may be stated precisely, e.g., maximum awareness by voters of positions taken by candidates for city offices on issues of policy expected to confront city officials. It may be established by the analysis that election of city officials at a time when national and state officials are not elected is a promising means to this end. But the reader of the analysis may be left unaware that the proposed means (separation of elections) may possibly have an adverse effect on something else he values, such as willingness of voters to go to the polls on election day or willingness of what he calls good people to engage in political activity. The reader, say the critics of our reform literature, is entitled not only to good means-ends analysis, but also to on-the-spot warning that the means may come at a higher price than he is willing to pay for that particular end.

Third, personal preference is permitted to intrude improperly in our reform literature. It intrudes in statements of ends when the political scientist mistakes his personal preferences for a widespread social demand. This appears to be what has happened in much of our writing about municipal home rule. Some of this literature creates the impression, if it does not state explicitly, that political leaders and opinion leaders in our great cities unite in a demand for home rule authority and are thwarted by powerholders who live outside the city. Contrary to what is suggested by this literature, the evidence seems generally to support a conclusion that leaders within the city are not united on this issue, and that the principal opposition to grant of home rule is provided by some of these urban leaders. It appears most likely that many political scientists who have written on this subject have projected their personal preferences into a community mind. If done consciously and deliberately this would appear to be an effort to win, by dishonest means, a hearing for the author's discourse which would not be accorded him if he truthfully stated the public valuation of the end he seeks to achieve.

Personal preference intrudes also in statements about the means by which particular ends can best be achieved. This appears to be what happens in argument that is palpably partial analysis, for example, in argument which plays up evidence that the proposed means will contribute to the desired end and understates or ignores evidence pointing to a contrary conclusion. It is possible, of course, that some writing of this character is a deliberate effort to deceive; it is much kinder to charge it to failure to recognize the force of personal preference or carelessness in identifying and disclosing personal preference.

Fourth, much of our reform literature, and possibly most of it, discloses a notable failure to meet minimum standards of proof in arriving at conclusions as to how an end may be achieved. This failure is due in large part to the intrusion of personal preference noted in the preceding paragraph. It stems also from inadequate appreciation of the complexity of social relationships. Our writing discloses too many failures to identify all the factors which contribute significantly to a social situation. The statement that acts A, B, and C will cause X to take place is faulty because it did not take into account another factor which makes act D necessary in order to arrive at X. Furthermore, there is failure to recognize that each change in a situation induces other changes. Acts A, B, C, and D each have consequences which complicate the advance toward X, and make necessary a series of acts beginning with E which must also be done in order to arrive at X. The recommendation of changes in institutions and the way things are done is a serious business. Someone pays a price for every change of even slightest social significance, and people ought not be advised to make changes until we can say with near-certainty that the anticipated gains will actually accrue. In the opinion of many political scientists, much of our literature applies standards of proof that are utterly inadequate for the responsibilities we assume in recommending changes.

For the alleged deficiencies which have been cited, the corrective undoubtedly lies in a fuller appreciation of the mood and mode of science and a stricter compliance with standards of scientific inquiry. Scientific method posits clear differentiation of things which are in fact different, comprehensiveness in establishing relevance, separation of preference from observations of objects and events, adherence to logic in reasoning, rigid compliance with standards and tests of proof found best by experience. Many political scientists find these characteristics of persuasive discourse missing from much of our literature that attempts to establish relationships between means and ends.

To the four deficiencies in our reform literature discussed above, I have encountered three pleas in defense.

One is a general disclaimer of the charges. When put in strongest terms, the defense is that little or none of our reform literature displays the deficiencies which have been cited. Other defenders of this literature acknowledge serious deficiencies but contend that the deficiencies are not serious enough to justify the castigation heaped upon this sector of our writings.

The *second* plea in defense asserts that the recommendations made in our reform literature are supported by a vast body of evidence not disclosed in our discourse and which need not be disclosed. Public experience in making and remaking institutions and in adopting and adapting ways of doing things has established many facts about means-ends relationships. The political scientist has knowledge of these findings and relies on them in his progress to conclusions; his failure to cite evidence so arrived at leads to false notions about the completeness of his analysis.

The *third* plea in defense argues, in effect, that poor guessing is better than no guessing. It is admitted that we recommend actions without being at all sure what consequences will flow out of the action, and it is admitted that we tell people what to do to achieve a goal before we find out whether the goal can more readily be achieved by other means. But we do the best we know how to do. And it is better for society to have such advice as we can offer than to have no advice. To counsel political scientists to propose no changes is to counsel society to make changes proposed by people whose guesses are less adequately supported by evidence than those which political scientists now make. We should certainly honor caution and seek to improve the quality of our study, say those who offer this defense, but we should not terminate our reform literature or refrain from giving advice until that far-distant day when we can meet the demands imposed by a rigorous scientific method.

CHAPTER X

How Shall We Treat Values?

It will not greatly misrepresent the actual state of affairs to say that two wings of the political science profession in this country wage a continuing battle on the issue of science vs. values. Like so many other controversies, this one can be partly erased by obtaining agreement on use of terms, especially on the meaning to be given the term "value." But the controversy is by no means wholly semantic. When there is agreement as to what should be called value, there remains a clash between conviction and commitment. The division into opposing camps begins with the very general question of whether we should study values at all, goes on to questions about what kind of study we should make (if we are going to study values) and what are the best methods of making such studies, and comes to its sharpest focus and greatest heat on questions about how to handle personal preference in scholarly literature. We shall examine the debate under three heads. (1) What is the legitimate place of values in political science? (2) What kinds of value study should we make? (3) How should personal preference be handled in scholarly writing?

WHAT IS THE LEGITIMATE PLACE OF VALUES IN POLITICAL SCIENCE?

This is an issue not to be settled in our time. The history of scholarly writing about values makes that an unavoidable conclusion. The most we can hope to do here is locate some main points where battle is joined and venture some judgments about why the combatants refuse to make peace. In such a venture the one who conducts the tour can easily get hurt, no matter how great his care to establish neutrality. I am reassured by some recent paragraphs of R. C. Pratt (No. 121 at pp. 373–74) which seem to confirm the position I take here. On the other hand, the slight resemblance of my own remarks to a very thoughtful analysis by Dwight Waldo (No. 8 at p. 96) makes me fear I may not have found out what the fighting is about.

What I have to say settles down to four general observations.

First, failure to agree on the place of values in the study of government and politics is in no small part due to differences in meaning which are put into the word "values." The narrowest meaning for the word makes it applicable only to something thought good for its own sake, to something which wholly supplies its own justification. Matters of this sort were called esthetic values earlier in this essay. Some people call them ultimate or final values.

But the term value is also given a very different application in our conversation and in our literature. In this usage, values are particular to the discourse. In one piece of writing the author examines alternative provisions for election of legislators, seeking to determine their effectiveness for achieving popular control of government. In this item of literature popular control of government is an end and electoral arrangements are means; we also say that in this particular discourse popular control of government is a value and the several provisions for electing legislators are not values. But in a second piece of writing, the author may have fixed as an end the establishment of government whose policies and acts are most widely and most readily complied with, and the purpose of his inquiry may be to determine whether popular control of government is an effective means for achieving this end. What was a value in the first item of literature is thus not a value in the second item. We can easily imagine other particular inquiries in which acceptability of governmental acts to publics is examined as possible means for still other ends, and imagine still other inquiries in which one or another specific arrangement for selecting legislators is viewed as an end and therefore, for that particular discourse, treated as a value.

It is readily seen that talk and writing about the place of values in our scholarly enterprise can become badly confused because of difference in the way "value" is used. The political scientist who says he wholly rejects values as a proper object of study may mean to say only that we ought not be concerned with ultimate, final, esthetic values. Or he may have in mind some earlier point where our inquiry ought to be cut off—any of a number of possible stopping points on the continuum of intermediate or instrumental values ranging from small matters commonly thought of only as means through more inclusive matters which are means in one discourse but ends in another. The same uncertainties exist about the intentions of political scientists who say study of values is a high-priority obligation for the profession. Such a person may intend to say that we should inquire into final, ultimate values. Or he too may have in mind a stopping point earlier on the continuum of instrumental values.

Second, in order to reduce or eliminate misunderstanding which arises out of different uses of the term, it is sometimes proposed that the word value be applied only to ends which are thought to provide their own justification; that things which are acknowledged to contribute to some other end never be called values. This recommendation receives support from some thoughtful individuals who have a strategic objective in mind. They fear that the word value, no matter what the specific referent, will call up in many minds all the implications of esthetic value. To call something a value is to invite the careless thinker to say: "I do not have to justify it. It is enough for you to know that my preferences, my tastes, my sense of right and wrong make it attractive to me. Don't ask me to prove that it is good or bad; values cannot be established by proof." But a thing, no matter how greatly cherished, which is a means to other ends can be justified by proof that it is an effective means to other ends which are also cherished. And no doubt many things which are treated in our literature as ends requiring no justification can be shown by thoughtful analysis to advance or to inhibit realization of other ends which are cherished more highly than this intermediate "value."

In the view of many political scientists, much of the literature produced by other political scientists falls into just this kind of trap. The searching inquiry into what a thing is valuable for, what it contributes to, where it stands in a structure of things valued—such a searching inquiry is avoided because what is actually a means to other ends is treated as if it were an end which provides its own justification. The word value thus becomes a refuge for laziness. A first step to purge our discipline of this refuge, it is argued, is to quit calling things values unless we first convince ourselves that the thing is not a means to other ends; that it does indeed supply its whole justification; that it is desirable for its own sake and not for the sake of something else.

Third, even when there is most careful effort to agree on use of terms, difficulty may arise because of different conceptions of the nature of value. Certainly many political scientists presume that ultimate, final, esthetic values exist and can be identified. Perhaps some who fall in this group are hopeful that the profession might generally agree as to what, for great numbers of people, these ultimate values are. Political scientists who are committed to an idea of ultimate values disagree among themselves as to whether values should be objects of inquiry for political scientists, or if values are inquired into, what kinds of inquiry ought to be made.

Dispute which starts within this sector of the profession is further complicated when issues are joined by those political scientists who reject the notion of ultimate values. I noted earlier (p. 110) my own doubt that one can identify any end which provides its whole justification and my own liking for the view that anything identifiable acquires its value from the support which it contributes to other things which are valued. I think it likely that a great many American political scientists are in a similar position. If so, they do not always make their position clear. Debate is not likely to advance understanding and alter conviction if it is carried on between parties, neither of whom knows quite what the other is talking about. This appears to be the case much of the time when the argument is about values in political science. Those on one side, taking for granted that everyone believes in ultimate values, fail to say where they stand on this matter; those on the other side doubt that ultimate values exist but do not bother to announce their unusual position.

Fourth, convictions about the proper place of values in political science are greatly affected by methodological commitments. The pro-science wing of the profession thinks political scientists are too much concerned about values; those who have least confidence in science as a way of studying human relationships think political scientists should continue or even increase their attention to values. I think it no exaggeration to say that the controversy about scientific emphasis in our study and the controversy about study of values are essentially one dispute, that science and values are opposite poles in a single area of intellectual conflict. (Cf. No. 38 at pp. 447–49.)

Our examination, in the next few pages, of controversy over these matters need not be tripped up by the variances in concepts and labelling of concepts discussed above. Some of the statements credited to protagonists in the following paragraphs may have specific application to values which are thought to provide their own justification; other statements, to values acknowledged to be instrumental. This will not generally be the case, however. Regardless of specific referents, the positions and contentions identified in the next paragraphs are, fundamentally, equally applicable to esthetic values and to those instrumental values which, though means to other ends, stand well up the continuum toward esthetic values.

Occasionally one hears a political scientist assert that he would absolutely exclude values from any consideration by political scientists, exclude them wholly and completely from consideration now and at any future time. Presumably he is thinking only of values which provide their own justification and not of instrumental values which are means to identifiable ends. Quite certainly, also, this is a man who thinks our highest duty, if not our only duty, is to make studies of a scientific character. Less extreme positions by those who would depress attention to values and step up the emphasis on scientific inquiry are revealed in statements like the following. "Writing which extols or deplores particular values and urges people to line up for or against particular values ought to be excluded from political science, but we ought to continue writing which identifies what men value, describes value systems, and provides value analysis." Or, "Identification of values, description of value systems, and value analysis are proper activities for political scientists now and in the future, but study directed to these objectives ought to be carried on in closest compliance with scientific method."

Or, "Study directed to these objectives is something we should get around to in the future, but such study is premature at this time because we have not yet developed proficiency in scientific study sufficient for effective analysis of such complicated packages of data."

I doubt that any political scientist denies the usefulness to society of literature directed to the three objectives differentiated above. The most any of them will ask for is that political scientists not engage in its production. The same goes for those who think study of values as ends is premature at this time, or think it is all right to go ahead with such study now if we confine our attention to what can be examined scientifically. They do not deny the usefulness to society of literature which extols and deplores, states personal preference, and issues calls to arms; they say only that certain kinds of writing have a legitimate place in political science and others do not. All these critics take their various positions because they think the primary, if not the whole, obligation of political scientists is to carry on studies which eventually settle questions by presentation of proof. Non-scientific inquiry, if widely practiced, diverts from our primary goal too much of the time of the few who are available for scholarly study of political science. Furthermore, extensive and serious preoccupation with non-scientific inquiry nurtures states of mind antagonistic to, if not wholly incompatible with, scientific inquiry. For one who believes these things it is a logical conclusion that political scientists will best serve the society that maintains them if they put aside a kind of writing that has up to now constituted a sizable part of their literature.

This reasoning naturally has little appeal for other political scientists whose methodological commitments are not those of science. Denying that study of legal governments should be limited to what science is good for, they see no reason for withdrawing attention from values, whether instrumental or esthetic. Political science has never been wholly confined or even mainly limited to scientific inquiry, they argue, and it will be a sad day if it ever becomes so restricted. Efforts to state what men value and why they value those things, extolling and deploring, and urging men to take their positions are a central concern of many of the writers whose work we honor as classics of political science. To terminate the stream of literature having this major purpose would be an act of mayhem which political scientists should be the last to propose. It has not been proven that a discipline cannot accommodate both scientific inquiry and extolling and deploring of values; if incompatibility of the two types of inquiry should be proven, it is at least arguable that we should continue inquiry into values and leave scientific studies to others.

WHAT KINDS OF VALUE STUDY SHOULD WE MAKE?

It is obvious that argument about whether political scientists should study values at all cannot get very far without going into questions of what kind of study should be made. The range of possible approaches to problems of value is too great for anything like a complete examination here. We shall confine our attention at this point to two centers of intellectual conflict: (1) the issue posed by the contention that study which attempts to identify values, describe value systems, or provide value analysis should meet the highest tests of scientific method; and (2) the issue posed by the contention that we place too little emphasis on value analysis. A third center of dispute is reserved for discussion in a separate major division of this chapter—writing in which particular values are extolled or deplored and in which people are urged to take their stand for or against particular values.

1. Scientific Study of Values

Political scientists who are attached to scientific method do not all line up in opposition to study of values. Many who

are in the pro-science wing of the profession insist that values
ought to be examined and that they can be examined in a
scientific way. The determination of what men value, the
description of value systems, and value analysis, they argue,
are best treated (or only treated well) by scientific study. To
find out what men value, you search for evidence. You find
out what men attach value to by examining their behavior
—what they do and what they say, what they do and what
they say put in relation to one another. Dependable, trustworthy descriptions of value systems rest on the same evidential base; you cannot know the total structure of a man's
values until you have established his position on particular
values and found out as a matter of fact how he accom-
modates particular values to one another. And you might find
out, if you search fully and carefully, that no one has a
constant value system; you might find that a man, caught up
in one set of circumstances, makes conscious decisions and
takes actions which enthrone certain values over others, and
later, caught up in a different set of circumstances, makes
conscious decisions and takes actions which arrange particular values in a different order of ascendancy and subjec-
tion. Finally, value analysis which tries to determine compatibilities and incompatibilities in values (which values
support and reinforce one another, which values impair and
hinder realization of others) also calls for examination of
evidence. You won't know what price you pay for freedom of
speech (one value) until you know in what ways and in what
degree freedom of speech contributes to anti-Semitic behavior and so impairs toleration of minority groups (another
value).

Political scientists who take the stand just set forth believe
that dependable, trustworthy statements about values as ends
can be supplied only by study which meets the tests of
scientific method. They think that too little (some may say
that none) of our current writing about values as ends arises

out of study that meets these tests. To the extent that current literature of this sort purports to rest on evidence and provide proof, it reveals contentment with a low quality of performance. If it is scientific study, it is sloppy scientific study.

The pleas of defense against this indictment are much the same as those noted above (pp. 172–173) for the defense of our reform literature. *One,* that our writing about values which rests on evidence as to what exists and occurs is better scientific performance than the critics admit. *Two,* that conclusions rest in good part on evidence taken into account by the writer but not disclosed to his reader. And *three* that the importance of the subject to society and its significance for other types of study by political scientists brand as irresponsible and remove from serious consideration a decision to put aside the study of values until the applications of scientific method to investigation of human relationships are more fully developed. People outside the political science profession, including philosophers and students of philosophy, also write inadequately about values, and the special preoccupations and knowledge of political scientists brings something of great usefulness to this body of literature. It is not required that we withhold our contributions until such later day as may find us in mastery of scientific method. It is only required that we be as nearly scientific as we now know how to be in areas of investigation where experience in science provides a guide. That standard we try to meet. If the best of our descriptive writing about values is sloppy science, our best counsel is to try to improve and not to quit.

2. Value Analysis

By value analysis I mean determination of compatibilities and incompatibilities among things valued and determination of how values support and reinforce one another or impair and hinder realization of one another. There is widespread dissatisfaction with our achievement in producing literature of this type. Dispute on this point may align the scientifically oriented against other political scientists, but it also divides political scientists who are alike in their lack of concern with being scientific.

It may be that our final goal in value analysis is nothing more nor less than elaborate description of value systems. That is, it may be that the best way to discover compatibilities and incompatibilities, reinforcements and impairments, is to make searching inquiry into how different values have actually been put together and brought into a balance by different persons or groups, how these structures of associated values are changed, how particular values rise to or fall from ascendancy over others, and so on. If one considers the objective in value analysis to be elaborate description, we may expect him to take the position that political scientists have done very little writing that is entitled to be called value analysis. Indeed, if the premise is granted, I think the conclusion must be accepted. We have produced few items which seriously attempt to describe a value system, and it is doubtful that any attempt that has been made meets a scientist's standard for elaborate description.

Dissatisfaction with our effort at value analysis is by no means confined to political scientists who think it is not sufficiently scientific. Many political scientists who are highly skeptical about the applicability of scientific method to human relationships think we have been too little concerned with value analysis and think that much of what is proffered as value analysis is too narrow in what it comprehends and too wanting in incisiveness to be given that classification. A variety of complaints which I have heard seem to me reducible to the general charge that we engage in one-line reasoning when we ought to engage in multiline reasoning.

What I call one-line reasoning characterizes, so I am told, much of the writing about civil rights which has appeared since World War II. The writer's discourse suggests, if he does not forthrightly declare, that freedom of expression (or privacy, or some other specified value) is so in ascendancy over all other values that there is no need to inquire whether it inhibits realization of other values. The writer thinks it sufficient to state why freedom of expression is good, indicating what other values it supports and reinforces; he affirms its compatibility with certain other values but he does not show an equal concern to find out whether it is wholly or partially incompatible with still other values, hindering their realization.

I presume that everything valued comes at some cost to other things which are also valued, and I have no doubt that all serious writing by political scientists reveals that they recognize this to be the case. The criticism of much of our literature is that it is too close to one-line reasoning; that compatibilities are overemphasized and incompatibilities are underemphasized. If anything said above suggests total failure to identify and put measures on incompatibilities, impairments, and hindrances, those statements can be toned down by the reader to indicate notable lack of adequacy in this respect. I say notable lack of adequacy because that is what I have many times heard said.

The correction for the notable lack of adequacy lies in what I have called multiline reasoning. Multiline reasoning does not preclude focus of attention and treatment which fixes, in a structure of values, the place of the value which is central to the discourse. I understand this is what Aristotle counseled us to do when he recommended a constant attention to *politeia,* a term which some political scientists prefer to translate as regime rather than the more frequent rendition as constitution. I understand the recent writings of Walter Berns to be a plea to remove freedom of expression from its splendid isolation and relocate it in a regime of competing values. See his *Freedom, Virtue, and the First*

Amendment (Louisiana State University, 1957), and his short essay (No. 66).

I have never heard or read a defense to the charge that we have put too little emphasis on value analysis. We may waive the rejoinder of the extreme pro-science members of the profession who would say that value analysis should not be attempted at all, or not be attempted at this time, and therefore that we have put too much emphasis on it. Perhaps some of those who count value analysis important would say that we have produced a great deal more of it than the critics seem to be aware of. I suspect that much of what will occur to many as defense of our achievements to date is more appropriate for the defense of personal preference statements than for the defense of what I have identified as value analysis. For that reason I think further consideration of intellectual conflict in this general area can best wait until we have noticed certain issues which arise in respect to preference writing.

HOW SHOULD PERSONAL PREFERENCE BE HANDLED IN SCHOLARLY WRITING?

Each item in a body of literature carries with it the special mark of the author. At risk of gross oversimplification I shall say that the author marks his product in three ways, and at risk of gross misuse of a word I shall call each of these an injection of personality. The author injects his personality into his product (a) by assumptions of risk, (b) by presumptions of knowledge, and (c) by incorporation of value preference. We shall be concerned here with the third of these, but because they are often confused with the third, a brief comment must be made on each of the first two.

Assumption of risk is illustrated as follows. I have limited resources for study of a problem. I might pursue study design A or design B but not both. I think A is more likely than B to pay off in findings, and I choose A. The decision is my response to risk. It is an expression of personality, and it has an impact on literature. Further illustration: I have carried my study as far as I can and have found alternative means to an end that appears to be socially desired. The evidence is inconclusive as to whether means A or means B is more certain to achieve the end. All considerations incidental to the two means cancel out. By guessing at unknowns I can put one means ahead of the other, and I do so. This is a response to risk which is an expression of personality and it has an effect on literature. I suspect there is hidden in our literature a lot of response to risk. Choices are made in response to risk, but the discourse at best does not disclose the act of risk; at worst it creates the impression that the writer thought the evidence induced the conclusion which he announced.

As to presumptions of knowledge, no one begins a study with a blank mind. Each student brings to his inquiry a pack of suppositions, beliefs, convictions which he calls knowledge. They are major determinants of his judgments about what to inquire into, what to look for, how to go about the search. Suppositions, beliefs, and convictions which are brought to the study supply tests by which new observations and inferences are evaluated, and provide an intellectual framework into which new accretions of knowledge will be fitted. This professional stock, this intellectual baggage, is peculiar to the individual; no one scholar carries quite the same equipment as any other. It is inevitable that these presumptions of knowledge will indelibly stamp the personality of the author on the product which results from his efforts.

The significance for development of literature of response to risk and presumptions of knowledge—especially the latter —would eminently repay careful investigation, but this is not the place for that inquiry. They are not at the center of intellectual conflict among political scientists at this time.

Controversy does abound, however, about the impact made upon our literature by injection of preference which is in response to value position.

Personal preference which is response to the writer's values may be injected into the discourse intentionally or unintentionally, boldly or timorously. It may be fully disclosed to the reader, or it may be scattered about so that the reader can detect its presence but cannot estimate its incidence, or it may be purposely concealed so as to cause the reader to suppose that proof has been provided when in fact evidence was lacking or ran the other way. Preference statements may take a form which makes values the center of attention, extolling and deploring particular values and calling men to line up for or against particular values. Or the writer's preferences may emerge in the discourse as the foundation of judgments about other matters—e.g., as premises in argument about what institutions and practices people will tolerate, or as explanation of why certain conceivable means were ignored in a search for effective means to a specified end.

I think we may presume that all political scientists admit that preference cannot be wholly excluded from scholarly work. The student is a man and he cannot make himself into a different man than he is. His own value commitments, those he is aware of plus those he is not aware of, are a part of his make-up. They help to determine what he gets interested in, what he chooses to look at, what he will see when he looks, and how he will evaluate what he sees. Opinions differ as to how fully we are in bondage to our values, what success we can attain when we try to identify and make allowances for them, what victories we can win when we struggle to suppress them. I suppose that differences in opinions on these matters contribute greatly to intellectual controversy about the way we handle values in discourse, but I have too little knowledge or conviction about this to attempt to relate it to the two issues which I shall discuss. The first issue relates to the aggrandizement of preference; the second to disclosure of preference.

1. Issue: Aggrandizement of Preference

The first issue is this: Should political scientists produce literature which is mainly, largely, or even in small degree designed to tell other people what the writer likes or what he thinks is good for society? I think the opposition to such writing was pretty well presented earlier in this discussion of values. It comes mainly if not altogether from political scientists who are devoted to scientific inquiry. They do not contend that such writing is injurious to society in general; they think it is injurious to political science as a discipline. They think the primary obligation of political scientists is to produce a different kind of discourse, and they think that preoccupation with preference statements both diverts men from more useful enterprise and fixes states of mind which inhibit production of more useful literature.

The defense of preference writing was only partially presented in earlier paragraphs. I think the full defense would stand on at least four grounds.

First, a point noted above, preference statements have always been a prominent part of the literature we call political science and their claim to legitimacy is therefore at least as great as the claim of scientific inquiry; there is no more reason for saying that preference writing should be terminated than there is for saying that political scientists should leave scientific investigation to other social study disciplines.

Second, statements of personal preference are helpful to other kinds of inquiry. The utopia is a case. When imagination is set free to ascertain how a particular set of values can be realized in institutions and practices, other students are provided with suggestions as to what may be worth looking into, what unsuspected relationships may lurk in institutions they previously supposed to have been fully explored, what untried means might be added to the list of instrumentalities available for the attainment of a variety of ends. It is not true to say that these aids to scholarship can be as well or better supplied by more objective inquiry. Efforts to restrain or exclude personal preference inevitably become a restraint on imagination. Enthusiasm for the task at hand unleashes powers of observation, of discrimination, of association and summation; enthusiasm brings unsuspected abilities to the aid of scholarship when one makes his boldest statements of what he likes and his most robust refutation or denunciation of what he does not like.

Third, society especially needs in our time the advice which political scientists give in statements of personal preference. Government today pervades virtually all of human affairs; it touches on everything men value. People cannot wait until science provides answers to their questions about how to use government to achieve a good life. They will act, and their acts will be shaped by the advice available to them. Thoughtful political scientists can provide better advice than other people on many things relating to government. This is because they have a more intense preoccupation with legal governments, have mastered a literature relating to legal governments, are intimately associated with people who make the study of legal governments their principal business. If political scientists do not boldly state what they like and dislike, and carefully support their positions by argument, society will fall victim to less well-informed and less thoughtfully established statements of preference.

Fourth, the notion that we can exclude personal preference from writing about legal governments is a delusion anyway. You can write about some matters relating to government with high hopes of excluding personal preference, but these matters are trivial in social significance. When you tackle matters of high significance, including most of the matters political scientists generally are committed to tackle, personal preference will intrude no matter how hard you try to exclude it. It is better to admit it freely to the discourse and honor the admission. The solution of our problems relating to personal preference is not in exclusion of preference statements; it lies in disclosure of what we like and dislike, and advice to the reader as to how he may allow for and correct against the writer's preferences.

2. Issue: Disclosure of Preference

We are thus brought to the second issue cited above, disclosure of preference. If we stand on the aphorism that "actions speak louder than words," I think we have to agree that some political scientists believe it is wholly proper for the writer to give his readers no clues to the preferences which affect the discourse, and even that it is proper to present what is really only wishful thinking in language which suggests that it is conclusion forced by evidence. I have not heard or read, and shall not attempt to contrive, a defense for these members of the profession.

We do verbalize differences of opinion as to what constitutes adequate disclosure of preference. I have not been able to identify standards or statements of ideals on which we divide. The dispute is directed to particular cases. We defend or condemn specific writings on the ground that they do or do not make adequate disclosure, or that they do or do not give adequate warning that preference intrudes where it cannot be disclosed. Since the dispute turns on specific cases rather than standards, I will make no effort to identify positions taken or to reproduce arguments pro and con. Some complaints and admonitions I have heard uttered are these.

He announced a conclusion which was one of several made tenable by the evidence. He should either have given all the alternatives equal status, or have produced evidence that one was more tenable than the others, or have admitted that he adopted one because his values made it more attractive to him.

He detailed the evidence in support of some of his conclusions but let other conclusions stand as fiat. The reader might suppose he had undisclosed evidence which supported the latter conclusions when in fact he had no such evidence. If he guessed his way to some of his conclusions he should have said so. If he arrived at some of his conclusions because he hoped that is the way things are, he should have said that he was influenced by personal preference.

He made uneven use of evidence, playing up that which supported his conclusions and ignoring or playing down evidence which ran to the contrary. If he didn't know what he was doing, he isn't fit to be in business. If he did it purposely, he should be run out of business.

He prejudiced the reader's ability to evaluate evidence by injecting into what appear to be objective descriptions sweet and sour words, laudatory comments, and crass or subtle aspersions. We assume enough risk when we present one side of an account without making an equal presentation of the other side. It is malpractice when we work on the emotions of the reader to pull his attention away from what we do not wish to present.

He could not possibly have told his readers how his personal preferences affected his discourse. But he could have stated in the preface the nature of the value system he brought to the study. If he could not describe his commitments, he could at least have acknowledged that he was prejudiced. If a man thinks he may be caught with his pants down, he should be the first to say that his pants are down.

CHAPTER XI

What Shall We Do with the Classics?

Snide remarks about social waste in maintaining political scientists who teach "political theory" and snide remarks about the intellectual depravity of political scientists who do not teach "political theory" have been in surplus supply at least ever since I was an undergraduate. There has been some evidence lately that the two sides to this hit-and-run war may come together soon in an actual joinder of issues. The issues on which we need to join and substitute wisdom for wit fall into two groups. First are questions about what the great writings provide that is useful to political scientists in our time. Second are questions about how best to exploit their useful contents.

On the *first* point, what the classic writings provide, the following seem to be the main possibilities. (a) They are models of intellectual effort, showing us what the great mind thought worthy of attention and how he dealt with it. (b) Collectively they record intellectual history, telling us what men have been concerned with over the years, revealing how persistent issues were examined, and recording continuing and changing beliefs. (c) They contain descriptions of ideologies, institutions, and practices which are useful today because applicable to life in our times. (d) They record findings born out of careful thought, accurate observation, and sophisticated research which provide a structure of knowledge we can extend by further inquiry. (e) They suggest problems and formulate and develop propositions which constitute hypotheses suitable for investigation by the best methods of proof and disproof available to us today.

On the *second* point, how to exploit what the classics provide, several courses of action are open to us. (a) We can have a division of labor, turning over to some political scientists the main or whole responsibility for studying the classics, for presenting their worth to undergraduate and graduate students, and for interpreting the great writings to other political scientists who study contemporary problems; or we can make it the obligation of all political scientists to utilize the classics, incorporating them into their teaching and exploiting their value for the studies we undertake. (b) In teaching the classics, we can make critical reading of the document our main concern; or fix main attention on the relation of the discourse to the life and times of the writer; or trace out a stream of literature, relating ideas to one another and showing development and change in ideas over periods of time and in response to events. (c) We can exploit the classics only as aids in examination of ideas and the planning and execution of empirical studies; or we can exploit them as models that challenge and instruct us (and our students) in mental projections which formulate normative doctrine and other imaginative structures (utopias).

I have no doubt that these two listings could be greatly extended, but meager as they are they provide a rich seedbed for controversy. Opinions can differ as to what the great writings actually contain or provide, the relevance and usefulness of these contents and provisions to contemporary political science, and best ways of extracting and applying whatever is there, is relevant, and is useful. Putting together in varying patterns the different positions people may take on each of these grounds, we can see that everybody who wants to get into the fight can have a special position which he shares with few other people. We shall not attempt to array the possible combinations here, but confine our discussion to three issue-centers where intellectual conflict is most heated. (1) Whether much of the content of the classics is relevant to and useful in political science. (2) Whether those who study and teach the classics (teachers of "political theory") adequately exploit their contents. (3) Whether political scientists who study contemporary problems and teach the other courses in political science adequately exploit the classics.

RELEVANCE AND USEFULNESS OF THE CLASSICS

It is readily apparent that we are presented with two points for division: (1) There will be differences of opinion as to what is relevant to and useful in political science. And (2) there will be differences of opinion as to what (and how much of it) the classic writings contain.

1. What Is Relevant and Useful?

The first question, what is relevant to and useful in political science, calls to attention again the dispute between those who are devoted to scientific inquiry and those who either reject scientific inquiry or think something in addition to scientific inquiry is required. Those pro-scientists who think we should not be concerned with esthetic values presumably will count as relevant to and useful in political science only that part of the content of the classics which is helpful in designing, executing, and checking further scientific inquiry. I have not heard or read a precise specification of things (kinds of statements) which the student who wishes only to do scientific study might hope to find in the classic literature. I suggest that he hopes to find these things.

(1) Comprehensive and incisive statement of what constitutes an ongoing political system. Such a statement would indicate what is central to politics; what is highly relevant, less relevant, and not relevant to politics; how things relevant, as components, are related together in the composition of a whole we can call a political system. I take it the contemporary student of politics, whether scientifically oriented or not, is guided in his inquiries by his notions of a political system, and his notions may be shaped and refined by the thought of men who struggled with this problem at any time in the past.

(2) Identification of questions, stated as hypotheses or convertible into hypotheses, suitable for verification or disproof by examination of evidence. Personal experience and acquaintance with contemporary literature and research activity will provide the student with more hypotheses than he can test. But good hypotheses, suitable for testing and significant to literature if tested, are arrived at in most cases after considerable studious effort. Thoughtful formulations in existing literature suggest precise hypotheses and help the contemporary student refine his own crude hypotheses.

(3) Thoughtful observations which instruct empirical inquiry. Helpful observations range from crude guesses as to relationships that would be found to exist if one made careful inquiry up to precise formulations of relationships which have been found to exist as a result of careful inquiry. In their fullest development, such observations constitute a body of theory, i.e., a series of generalizations all of which have relevance to the same matter, and which collectively postulate the existence of things not readily apparent to the observer or indicate relationships among the several factors in a situation. Theory and other thoughtful observations which arise out of familiarity with the real world and which relate to the real world (i.e., which have empirical reference) help the student formulate his objective of inquiry, design his

research, evaluate his findings, and relate his findings to the findings of other students.

(4) Accurate descriptions of real situations. As illustration, the believed-to-be accurate account, no matter when made, of how some men in other times and other places gained advantage over other men suggests to the present-day student some possibilities in advantage-getting which he may wish to investigate in the situations he explores, and provides him with a body of data and findings against which he may check his own data and findings. Furthermore, the literature of descriptive accounts cumulates. When we have examined a sizable sample of situations having enough in common, we may offer some generalizations about what seems most likely to occur, other things being equal. The believed-to-be accurate accounts of previous writers may thus combine with the believed-to-be accurate accounts of contemporary and future students to provide a literature that approaches scientific character.

I suppose that virtually all contemporary political scientists, including those who take the dimmest view of scientific study of human relationships, will agree that each of the four types of content listed in the preceding paragraph are relevant to and useful in political science and should be utilized if we can find them in the classic writings. In addition, those who are not scientifically oriented find a wide range of other matters relevant and useful. I have been told that some members of our profession count everything in the classics relevant and useful because their notion of what is relevant to and useful in political science is fixed by what they find in the writings they were told in their youth are classics of political literature. Speaking for those who form their judgments on other grounds and are critical of the classic literature, I presume they would add the following to the foregoing list of things relevant to and useful in political science.

(5) Inquiry into values. As noted earlier, many American political scientists extend the assignment of political science to include inquiry into ultimate or esthetic values, why certain value-laden goals are thought worthy of achievement, and how things valued support and reinforce one another or impair and hinder realization of one another. Those who take this position accordingly attach great importance to thoughtful writing about values in the classic literature.

(6) Statements of personal preference. No doubt the forgotten literature of the past abounds in statements of what the author liked and did not like, and why he thought other people ought to share his likes and dislikes. The remembered statements of preference which we honor as classics are honored for one or both of two reasons. We read them today because they are fully developed, at least challenging to our generation, and possibly convincing; or we read them because they represent the position of a man who is honored because of his other contributions to great literature. The most thoughtful of the highly developed preference statements are models. They tell us more than that one man believed this; we read them as evidence of what other men believed, presented in a form more perfect than any but a few men could achieve. They are for contemporary students of value and value systems data to be examined and incorporated in present-day study, and they are guides for thoughtful analysis of problems relating to value and value systems.

(7) Speculative discourse. As was pointed out in Chapter IX, the hardest core of scientific literature includes speculative discourse, for imagination runs beyond observation to identify objectives of inquiry and set up theory to guide inquiry and check findings. When we come to a barrier in the search for evidence, we extrapolate selected experiences and reason from analogues. Some discourse is so heavy with imaginative projections (I call it speculation) and so meager in reference to observation that the scientist counts it worth-

less. Many political scientists find usefulness in speculative discourse which other political scientists, more concerned to be scientific, discard as of no worth. Insight thus becomes a key word in current dispute. Political Scientist A says that the great writer gave us the benefit of a remarkable insight into why men do what they do; Political Scientist B suspects that the great writer had no evidence to support his conclusion, that he made the rankest kind of guess, and that he was presumptuous to offer so unfounded a guess for serious consideration by other people.

Reasoning from what I know about contemporary study, I conclude that evidence-supported conclusions are harder to come at in respect to values and value systems than in respect to most other areas of our inquiry. If this is so, we may expect those political scientists who engage in value study to place more reliance on speculative discourse than will political scientists with other interests. Frustrated in their effort to find the evidence they seek, they are forced to resort to speculation as a means of filling gaps resulting from lack of sufficient evidence. Finding speculation essential to their own discourse, they necessarily attach great importance to thoughtful speculation of writers who went before. I suspect that they are more liberal than other political scientists in honoring speculation relating to matters which lend themselves to verification by examination of evidence.

2. What Do the Classics Contain?

This question apparently cannot be answered simply by reading the documents to see what the great men had to say. I have listened to argument among men who make study and teaching of "political theory" their main preoccupation, and they disagree as to whether there is a great deal or only a little bit in the classics of one or more types of content listed in the preceding paragraphs. I conclude that there is no important disagreement about the last three items in the list of seven. I think all students of the classics acknowledge that there is extensive discussion of values and value systems, fully and carefully developed statements of personal preference, and extensive speculation running far beyond reported evidence. It appears to be agreed also that political scientists who attach importance to these kinds of discourse can find rich rewards in the literature we treat as classic. I conclude that there is like agreement that the classics supply many extended statements, and highly useful statements, of what constitutes an ongoing political system, the first item in the list. Opinions may differ as to whether the contemporary student needs to go back to the classics for instruction on this point; there is agreement that they provide instruction as to what are the parts of a whole, and how the parts are combined to make a whole political system.

As to the remaining items in the list, I must report sharp disagreement. I have heard one man say, "The classics are rich with hypotheses ripe for verification or disproof," and heard another man retort, "Show me a couple!" I have heard assertion and denial that the present-day student who searches the real world for evidence can find, in the classics, highly suggestive guides for his research, highly developed bodies of theory which he can put in operation in his research, model empirical inquiries which he may closely follow in designing and executing his own research. There is also dispute as to how much there is in the classics of believed-to-be accurate descriptions of real situations. That there are some reliable and revealing descriptions of institutions, of practices, and of belief systems I think all will agree. But there is disagreement as to whether there is much or only a little of it.

I conclude, after listening to the argument, that much of the dispute turns not on what the great men said but on what is the import for further study of the things they said. One political scientist says, "Here is a firm hypothesis offered by

Locke (or Rousseau, or Mill); why don't you fellows test it?" and the man addressed answers, "Obviously you don't have the slightest understanding of what is a testable hypothesis." One political scientist says, "Here is an accurate description of a real situation," and he gets the answer "I see evidence of guesswork scattered all through it."

I am relieved of temptation to offer my own judgments on the matters in dispute by my certain knowledge that I have not examined nearly all the writings we call great. I am confident that those who wish to explore the usefulness of the great writers for contemporary empirical research will gain from reading the essay by Mulford Sibley on "The place of classical political theory in the study of politics" (No. 8). Less accessible is a paper by Norton Long entitled "Aristotle and the study of local government" (read before American Political Science Association, Boulder, Colorado, September, 1955).

EXPLOITATION BY "THEORY" TEACHERS

Given great disagreement about what is of current usefulness in the classics, one must expect great disagreement as to whether their usefulness is exploited by those who study and teach the classics. The study and teaching of classic literature has recently come in for severe criticism, in some cases severe enough to be called castigation (see No. 25).

Some political scientists who would use the classic writings as aids for contemporary scientific inquiry indict the teachers of "political theory" for failure to exploit that content of the classics which is useful to the scientist. There are fruitful hypotheses suitable for testing in the great writings, they say, but the teachers of "political theory" either ignore them completely or do not sufficiently emphasize and explain their usefulness. There are reliable descriptions and thoughtful analyses of things which have their counterparts in our own times, but the teachers of "political theory" do not relate these earlier studies to contemporary research and writing. Instead of rescuing these useful materials so that they may have a career, the "political theory" teachers let them go unnoticed while they give attention to other expressions which, because of their character, cannot have a career in ongoing science.

I do not know what happens in classrooms, but I conclude that the charge is a true statement of facts insofar as it applies to published writings by men who specialize in study of the classic literature. It does not of necessity follow, however, that the teachers of "political theory" are guilty of offense. I think we may assume that people who take the classics as their objects of study are not likely to carry on rigorous empirical research as a sideline. If few, or none, of them are motivated to do scientific inquiry themselves, it is hardly to be expected that they will comb a literature to find out what it offers for a type of research they are not themselves interested in doing. The classics contain discourse which is highly relevant to types of inquiry and to objectives of study which are attractive to the "theory" teachers; it is not surprising that they exploit this part of the content and neglect that which is most relevant to scientific inquiry. Their choice of what to exploit does not bar the content relevant to science from its rightful place in an ongoing science. The political scientist who would prove himself to be a scientist can read the classics himself and extract what he finds useful for his own purposes; if he is also a teacher, he can make the classics required reading in his own courses and he can extract and interpret to his students what he thinks they might not adequately understand on their own reading. We shall consider this point under the next main section of this chapter.

Dissatisfaction with study and teaching of the classics is not confined to political scientists who are scientifically oriented. The most severe criticisms I have seen in print are by men who themselves are teachers of courses called political theory. The criticism which comes from this branch of the profession may include a charge that the materials relevant to science are neglected, but it goes beyond this point to make a broadside indictment specifying failure to exploit the great writings for any useful present-day purpose.

Very few students and teachers of "political theory," runs the indictment in its strongest form, are analysts of ideas or critics of the literature they study. Very few of them attempt to extract from the great writing what is relevant to and significant for present-day study, to interpret the great man's words so as to make readily apparent the range of their relevance and the sharpness of their significance, to extend the analysis which the great man made for his time by bringing into the analysis considerations he did not or could not have taken into account. Instead of acting as analysts (extracting, interpreting, extending) and delivering to literature in the making what great writers of the past surely provided, those who study and teach the classics have turned themselves into historians who identify origins of ideas, relate writers and their ideas to the times that influenced the writer and shaped his ideas, and describe a stream of literature by relating to one another different writers, different ideas, and successive developments in particular ideas.

Furthermore, the indictment continues, teachers of "political theory" not only fail to deliver the wisdom of the classics in their own writings addressed to mature students of political science; they do not use the classics effectively in training their students. In most "political theory" courses the main assignment is a textbook and the student spends far more time reading about great writers and great literature than he spends reading what the great writers actually said. Only by reading the original document can the young man learn how the great man identified a significant objective of inquiry, defined and refined his area of concern, searched for evidence and evaluated evidence, resorted to extrapolations and analogues as substitutes for evidence where evidence appeared unobtainable, and utilized reasoning to glue the components of his knowledge into a persuasive whole. To study them as models of discourse under the critical supervision of a mature student and teacher is the greatest value which the classics have for the young man studying political science. So runs the indictment in its extreme form.

Again I have to report that I have not heard or read a fully developed denial of the charges or plea of defense. This much I have encountered.

First, that the charges are greatly exaggerated or wholly false. "I and other teachers of political theory do try to be analysts; we do the best we know how in extracting the useful, interpreting it, applying it to present scholarly preoccupations, extending the analysis beyond the point where the great man left it. And we do make our students read the original documents. Approved practice requires the undergraduate student to read at least one classic writing in its entirety, and at least to read segments of other items of great discourse. But this is not enough, for the great discourse does not stand isolate from the times in which it was produced or from the discourse which preceded it, was companion to it, and succeeded it. We do not assign the textbook in order to make study of great literature more palatable or less fatiguing. We assign the textbook because it enhances the value gained from reading the document itself."

Second, in the reply: "You ask too much of the teacher of political theory. The job of making available the wisdom in the great writings is a job for all political scientists, not just a job for men who direct attention mainly to the classics. If what Milton and Mill said about liberty and freedom of expression is not adequately exploited in study and teaching today, the failure is chargeable to the men who study and teach contemporary politics and constitutional law as well as the men who teach political theory."

Third: "If what we mainly do is historical inquiry, it is historical inquiry that needs to be made and is best made by men trained in political science. Ideas are not mere verbalizations. The great writer did not say everything that he intended to have understood. He wrote with reference to a world of events, and he expected those events to be in the mind of his reader and projected by the reader into the discourse. If we ignore the social context of the writing, we make some of the great writers look naïve if not foolish; if we relate the times to the writing we discover imagination, wit, and wisdom. Since the writings we study deal with politics, the man who is trained for study of politics is more likely than men with other training to disclose the high merit that surely characterizes the classic. By serving as historian of ideas, the political scientist who is student and teacher of political theory interprets the great writer and delivers to present-day students the wisdom in his words that would otherwise have escaped us."

EXPLOITATION BY STUDENTS OF CONTEMPORARY POLITICS

We must now put a shoe on another big foot. The teachers of "political theory" indict the rest of the political science profession. They say (1) that many political scientists reveal in their conversation, and some frankly admit, that they do not know what is in the classics; (2) that many political scientists who say there is useful content in the classics and who criticize students and teachers of "political theory" for not bringing it out do not themselves exploit the classics in their study and teaching; and (c) that those who study contemporary problems and teach the courses which are not labelled "political theory" are primarily responsible for the breach between past and present study of politics because, if an effective union is to be made, it must be made right in the study which tackles contemporary problems and in the teaching which prepares young people to study contemporary problems.

I think we must acknowledge the truth of the first two charges. I have certainly heard many political scientists say that they do not know what is in the classics—that they did not have a good course in "political theory" in their undergraduate or graduate days and that they have not got around to a reading of the classics since. Some political scientists who have made this confession in my presence added that they doubt there is much of usefulness for political science in the classics, but many others asserted a faith that usefulness is there and admitted a supposition that they suffer because they have missed something. Furthermore, my own reading of contemporary writing by American political scientists in subject areas that I claim to know most about convinces me that very few of them make a conscious effort to relate the statements of the classic writers to their own discourse. If they are influenced by the classics, it must be admitted that they make little effort to disclose it; the great man's words rarely appear between quotation marks and the titles of his books rarely appear in footnotes. What the facts are on these matters need not worry us further here; if my own testimony and that of the "political theorists" who criticize the rest of us seems exaggerated, we nevertheless can expect general agreement that a great many political scientists do not make a conscious effort to incorporate the classic literature into their teaching and their study of contemporary problems.

The remaining charge in the indictment requires more extended comment—that the effective union of classic scholarship and present-day scholarship must be made in current study and the training of young men for such study, and that if the political scientists who carry on that study and provide that training do not make use of the classics, they must bear the brunt of blame for the breach between classic and present-day scholarship. The complaint, supported by illustrations, reads as follows.

If, as Norton Long argues, utilization of certain concepts and points of view found in Aristotle would greatly improve our studies of local government, it is the political scientists who study local government and teach courses in local government that should make the application. They are not excused on the pleading that the men who taught them "political theory" in their youth did not show the relevance of Aristotle to local government studies; there is no statute of limitations on extending one's education.

If Montesquieu was partly right and partly wrong, partly wise and partly foolish about separation of powers, the best time to impress students with his wisdom and show them where he fell into error is right in the courses where they study the formation of our constitution and examine the current operations of a government of three branches. Right when the student is studying the debate between men charged with designing a government or studying the practical problems of making it work to general satisfaction is the moment when the student sees highest relevance in Montesquieu's model and is best able to appraise the adequacy of his analysis.

Professor George Sabine argues persuasively (No. 123) that there are two great democratic traditions, significantly different, which largely shape governmental institutions and structure political activity in what we currently call the free world; that you best understand one tradition if you read Rousseau carefully and you best understand the other if you read Locke with equal care. Some political science departments have courses which make analysis of democracy or democratic government the primary or whole concern; all departments have courses which examine governmental organization and political practices in terms of democratic presumptions. If Professor Sabine is right that Rousseau and Locke are prime expositors of competing democratic theories, why aren't Rousseau and Locke required reading in these courses? Is the student in the course titled Political Parties expected to have read Rousseau and Locke beforehand? Or does the professor think these men didn't have much to say? Or does the professor not know that there are at least two significantly different democratic traditions against which provision for elective offices, party organization, and political practices may be tested?

I presume most American political scientists who teach the courses not labelled political theory will agree that the facts are as alleged above. I have heard that some departments start the student on his way through a major in political science by a reading of classic literature, but I have no doubt that far more of the country's seniors majoring in political science can identify Ogg and Ray, or Burns and Peltason, or Swarthout and Bartley than can name a book written by Plato or Aristotle, Hobbes or Locke, Montesquieu or Rousseau. I do not remember seeing Aristotle's concepts and points of view set forth in any textbook offered for sale to students taking courses called local government. I looked in nine leading textbooks offered for courses called Political Parties; I found Rousseau and Locke listed in the indexes of two, Rousseau but not Locke in the indexes of two, and neither Rousseau nor Locke in the indexes of the remaining five. I do not know how far the teachers of courses on Political Parties may run ahead of the more prosperous members of the profession who write textbooks for them, but if many of them require their students to read the classics as part of their course assignments they have not mentioned it in my presence. I can say the same thing about the teachers of local government (municipal or rural or both), teachers of public administration, teachers of constitutional law, teachers of international politics, teachers of courses on foreign systems other than Russia where Marx may be assigned but probably no other ancient great.

Admitting the charge, what is the defense?

First is the reply of those who say there is nothing worthwhile for present-day study in the great writers. If they believe this, they need make no further defense of their exclusion of the classics; you may reject the man but you cannot honor the man and reject his defense.

Second, I have heard a number of political scientists say in effect: There is wisdom in the great writings and I honor the great writers for towering so high above their contemporaries. They repay reading when you can find the time for it. But reading what they wrote is as respects most of them an uneconomical way of incorporating their wisdom. The things they provide which are useful in current study have been incorporated in the more recent literature we assign to our students, sometimes with credit in a footnote but more often as unacknowledged appropriation of ideas in the public domain. There is a lot of nonsense in the *Social Contract,* and you can't assign pages which catch all the wisdom and exclude all the nonsense. Machiavelli introduced some keen observation and hard common sense into the literature of politics, but you can find more stuff and better stuff of his kind in any good daily newspaper which the student ought to read anyway. Hobbes ought to be read, but not read as an assignment in a course which deals with problems of government and politics today. Every political science major ought to read *Leviathan* from start to finish to see how a great mind conceived and described a political system; but the best way to give him that experience is in a course where a few of the great writings are examined with the guidance of a teacher whose whole purpose is to impress on his students how great minds produced the great works that came out of them.

I doubt that anything would be gained from my effort to examine the argument in greater detail. I suspect that if the argument is extended in other places, a great many teachers of "political theory" and quite a few political scientists who do not teach "political theory" will persist in the belief that much of the wisdom in the classics is not passing directly or by indirect route into most of our courses. I suspect they will also persist in the belief that most political scientists reveal in their writing that they have not incorporated the wisdom of the great writers into their own minds. But I think it equally likely that a substantial number of political scientists will continue to doubt that the classics provide much that is useful for current scholarship and teaching; that many who ascribe great value to the classics will still contend that they have made a studied effort to capture and utilize it; and that still other political scientists will persist in the conviction that about everything of importance which the great writers have to offer has crept, noticed or unnoticed, into our textbooks, into our lectures, and into the writing which we offer as our contribution to a scholarly literature.

REFERENCES

The numbered items are cited in the text by number only. Additional items which examine the state of political science as discipline and profession appear at the end of this list.

I. COLLECTIONS OF ESSAYS

1. *Contemporary Political Science.* (UNESCO Publication No. 426.) Liege: 1950.
2. Eulau, Heinz, Eldersveld, Samuel J., and Janowitz, Morris (eds.). *Political Behavior: A Reader in Theory and Research.* Glencoe, Ill.: The Free Press, 1956.
3. Lerner, Daniel, and Lasswell, Harold D. *The Policy Sciences.* Stanford: Stanford University, 1951.
4. *Research Frontiers in Politics and Government.* Washington: Brookings Institution, 1955.
5. Rice, Stuart A. (ed.). *Methods in Social Sciences: A Case Book.* Chicago: University of Chicago Press, 1931.
6. Siffin, William J. (ed.). *Toward the Comparative Study of Public Administration.* Bloomington: Department of Government, Indiana University, 1957.
7. Snyder, Richard C. (ed.). *Short Studies in Political Science.* New York: Doubleday, 1955.
   7a. No. 1. Karl Deutsch, *Political Communication at the*

International Level; Problems of Definition and Measurement.

7b. No. 11. Dwight Waldo, *The Study of Public Administration.*

7c. No. 21. Roy C. Macridis, *The Study of Comparative Government.*

7d. No. 25. Jack W. Peltason, *Federal Courts in the Political Process.*

7e. No. 26. Neil A. McDonald, *The Study of Political Parties.*

8. Young, Roland (ed.). *Approaches to the Study of Politics.* Evanston, Ill.: Northwestern University Press, 1958.

II. ARTICLES IN *AMERICAN POLITICAL SCIENCE REVIEW*

9. Almond, Gabriel A., Cole, Taylor, and Macridis, Roy C. "A suggested research strategy in Western European government and politics," 49 (1955), 1042.

10. Apter, David E. "Theory and the study of politics," 51 (1957), 747.

11. Berdahl, Clarence A. "Party membership in the United States," 36 (1942), 16, 241.

12. Campbell, Angus, Gurin, Gerald, and Miller, Warren E. "Political issues and the vote: November, 1952," 47 (1953), 359.

13. Campbell, Angus, and Miller, Warren E. "The motivational basis of straight and split ticket voting," 51 (1957), 293.

14. Dahl, Robert A. "A critique of the ruling elite model," 52 (1958), 463.

15. Daland, R. T. "Political science and the study of urbanism," 51 (1957), 491.

16. Davies, James C. "Charisma in the 1952 campaign," 48 (1954), 1083. Reprinted in No. 2 above.

17. Eckstein, Harry. "Political theory and the study of politics: a report of a conference," 50 (1956), 475.

18. Eldersveld, Samuel J. "The independent vote: measurement,

characteristics, and implications for party strategy," 46 (1952), 732.

19. Eulau, Heinz. "Perceptions of class and party in voting behavior: 1952," 49 (1955), 364. Reprinted in No. 2 above.

20. Feeley, James K., Jr. "An analysis of administrative purpose," 45 (1951), 1069.

21. Field, G. Lowell. "Law as an objective political concept," 43 (1949), 229.

22. Fisher, Franklin M. "The mathematical analysis of Supreme Court decisions: the use and abuse of quantitative methods," 52 (1958), 321.

23. Garceau, Oliver. "Research in the political process," 45 (1951), 69. Reprinted in No. 2 above.

24. Haas, Ernst B. "Types of collective security; an examination of operational concepts," 49 (1955), 40.

25. Hacker, Andrew. "Capital and carbuncles: the 'Great Books' reappraised," 48 (1954), 775.

26. Herson, Lawrence J. R. "The lost world of municipal government," 51 (1957), 330.

27. Jewell, Malcolm E. "Party voting in American state legislatures," 49 (1955), 773.

28. Kahin, George McT., Pauker, Guy J., and Pye, Lucian W. "Comparative politics of non-Western countries," 49 (1955), 1022.

29. Kaufman, Herbert. "Emerging conflicts in the doctrine of public administration," 50 (1956), 1057.

30. Keefe, William J. "Parties, partisanship, and public policy in the Pennsylvania legislature," 48 (1954), 450.

31. Kenyon, Cecilia M. "Where Paine went wrong," 45 (1951), 1086.

32. Kort, Fred. "Predicting Supreme Court decisions mathematically: a quantitative analysis of the 'right to counsel' cases," 51 (1957), 1.

33. ———. "Reply to Fisher's *Mathematical analysis of Supreme Court decisions*," 52 (1958), 339.

34. Lane, Robert E. "Political personality and electoral choice," 49 (1955), 173.

35. Lasswell, Harold D. "The immediate future of research policy and method in political science," 45 (1951), 133.

36. ———. "The political science of science," 50 (1956), 961.

37. Lockard, W. Duane. "Legislative politics in Connecticut," 48 (1954), 166.

38. Macpherson, C. B. "World trends in political science research," 48 (1954), 427.

39. MacRae, Duncan, Jr. "The relation between roll call votes and constituencies in the Massachusetts House of Representatives," 46 (1952), 1046. Reprinted in No. 2 above.

40. March, James G. "Introduction to the theory and measurement of influence," 49 (1955), 431. Reprinted in No. 2 above.

41. Marz, Roger H. "*The Democratic Digest:* a content analysis," 51 (1957), 696.

42. Miller, Warren E. "Party preference and attitudes on political issues: 1948–1951," 47 (1953), 45.

43. ———. "One party politics and the voter," 50 (1956), 707.

44. Oppenheim, Felix E. "Interpersonal freedom and freedom of action," 49 (1955), 353.

45. Penniman, Howard. "Thomas Paine—democrat," 37 (1943), 244.

46. Pennock, J. Roland. "Responsiveness, responsibility, and majority rule," 46 (1952), 790.

47. Prothro, James W. "Verbal shifts in the American presidency: a content analysis," 50 (1956), 726. Comment by Howard B. White follows at p. 740.

48. Riggs, Fred W. "Notes on literature available for the study of comparative public administration," 48 (1954), 515.

49. Riker, William H. "The paradox of voting and congressional rules for voting on amendments," 52 (1958), 349.

50. Rockwell, Landon G. "Toward a more integrated political science curriculum," 41 (1947), 314.

51. Rogow, Arnold A. "Comment on Smith and Apter: or, Whatever happened to the great issues?" 51 (1957), 763.
52. Schubert, Glendon A., Jr. "The public interest in administrative decision-making: theorem, theosophy, or theory?" 51 (1957), 346.
53. Shields, Currin V. "The American tradition of empirical collectivism," 46 (1952), 104.
54. Simon, Herbert A. "Comments on the theory of organization," 46 (1952), 1130.
55. Smith, David G. "Political science and political theory," 51 (1957), 734.
56. Spitz, David. "Democracy and the problem of civil disobedience," 48 (1954), 386.
57. Starr, Joseph R. "The legal status of American political parties," 34 (1940), 439, 685.
58. Stokes, Donald, Campbell, Angus, and Miller, Warren E. "Components of electoral decisions," 52 (1958), 367.
59. Thompson, Kenneth W. "Toward a theory of international politics," 49 (1955), 733.
60. Truman, David B. "The state delegations and the structure of party voting in the United States House of Representatives," 50 (1956), 1023.
61. Waldo, Dwight. "Development of theory of democratic administration," 46 (1952), 81. Commentary on this article follows on p. 494.
62. Wollin, Sheldon S. "Hume and conservatism," 48 (1954), 999.
63. "Research in comparative politics: report of a seminar," 47 (1953), 641. Followed by comments on the report by Carl J. Friedrich, Harold D. Lasswell, Herbert A. Simon, Ralph J. D. Braibanti, G. Lowell Field, and Dwight Waldo.
64. "Research in political behavior," 46 (1952), 1003. Reprinted in No. 2 above.

III. ARTICLES IN JOURNAL OF POLITICS

65. Almond, Gabriel A. "Comparative political systems," 18 (1956), 391. Reprinted in No. 2 above.

66. Berns, Walter. "Freedom and loyalty," 18 (1956), 17.

67. Beth, Loren P. "The case for judicial protection of civil liberties," 17 (1955), 100.

68. Easton, David. "The decline of modern political theory," 13 (1951), 36.

69. ————. "Harold Lasswell: policy scientist for a democratic society," 12 (1950), 450.

70. Eldersveld, Samuel J. "Theory and method in voting behavior research," 13 (1951), 70. Reprinted in No. 2 above.

71. Engelmann, Frederick G. "A critique of recent writings on political parties," 19 (1957), 423.

72. Farris, Charles D. "A method of determining ideological groupings in the Congress," 20 (1958), 308.

73. Haas, Ernst B. "The balance of power as a guide to policy-making," 15 (1953), 370.

74. Humphrey, Robert L. "The theory of international relations," 17 (1955), 664.

75. Kendall, Willmoore. "Prolegomena to any future work on majority rule," 12 (1950), 694.

76. Latham, Earl. "The Supreme Court and the supreme people," 16 (1954), 207.

77. Lippincott, Benjamin E. "The bias of American political science," 2 (1940), 125.

78. McClosky, Herbert. "The fallacy of absolute majority rule," 11 (1949), 638.

79. Mendelson, Wallace. "The degradation of the clear and present danger rule," 15 (1953), 349.

80. Neumann, Sigmund. "Comparative politics: a half-century appraisal," 19 (1957), 369. Commentary on this article follows on pp. 479, 485.

81. Oppenheim, Felix E. "Analysis of political control: actual and potential," 20 (1958), 515.

82. Prothro, James W. "The nonsense fight over scientific method: a plea for peace," 18 (1956), 565.

83. Pye, Lucian W. "The non-Western political process," 20 (1958), 468.

84. Shepard, Max A. "An analysis of analytical jurisprudence," 1 (1939), 371.

85. Simon, Herbert A. "Notes on the observation and measurement of political power," 15 (1953), 500.

86. Smithburg, Donald W. "Political theory and public administration," 13 (1951), 59.

87. Sorauf, Frank F. "The public interest reconsidered," 19 (1957), 616.

88. Turner, Julius. "Primary elections as the alternative to party competition in safe districts," 15 (1953), 197.

89. White, Leonard D. "Political science, mid-century," 12 (1950), 13.

IV. ARTICLES IN *PUBLIC ADMINISTRATION REVIEW*

90. Dahl, Robert A. "The science of public administration; three problems," 7 (1947), 1.

91. Edelman, Murray. "Governmental organization and public policy," 12 (1952), 276.

92. Grodzins, Morton. "Public administration and the science of human relations," 11 (1951), 88. Reprinted in No. 2 above.

93. Kaufman, Herbert, and Jones, Victor. "The mystery of power," 14 (1954), 205.

94. Lewis, Verne B. "Toward a theory of budgeting," 12 (1952), 42.

95. Long, Norton E. "Power and administration," 9 (1949), 257.

96. ————. "Public policy and administration: the goals of rationality and responsibility," 14 (1954), 22.

97. Maas, Arthur A., and Radway, Laurence I. "Gauging administrative responsibility," 9 (1949), 182.

98. Richards, Allan R. "Local government research: a partial evaluation," 14 (1954), 271.

99. Simon, Herbert A. "A comment on 'The science of public administration,'" 7 (1947), 200.

V. ARTICLES IN OTHER JOURNALS

100. Agger, Robert E. "Power attributions in the local community: theoretical and research consideration," *Social Forces*, 34 (1956), 321.

101. Ash, Maurice. "An analysis of power with special reference to international politics," *World Politics*, 3 (1951), 218.

102. Bierstedt, Robert. "An analysis of social power," *American Sociological Review*, 15 (1950), 730.

103. Catlin, George. "Political theory: What is it?" *Political Science Quarterly*, 72 (1957), 1.

104. Cook, Thomas I. "The political system: the stubborn search for a science of politics," *Journal of Philosophy*, 51 (1954), 128.

105. Dahl, Robert A. "The concept of power," *Behavioral Science*, 2 (1957), 201.

106. Dotson, Arch. "Fundamental approaches to administrative responsibility," *Western Political Quarterly*, 10 (1957), 701.

107. Epstein, Leon D. "British mass parties in comparison with American parties," *Political Science Quarterly*, 71 (1956), 97.

108. Haas, Ernst B. "The balance of power: prescription, concept, or propaganda," *World Politics*, 5 (1953), 442.

109. Kaplan, Morton. "The international arena as a source of dysfunctional tension," *World Politics*, 6 (1953), 501.

110. Keefe, William J. "Party government and lawmaking in the Illinois General Assembly," *Northwestern University Law Review*, 47 (1952), 55.

111. LaPalombara, Joseph. "Political party systems and crisis governments: French and Italian contrasts," *Midwest Journal of Political Science*, 2 (1958), 117.

112. Leiserson, Avery. "Problems of methodology in political research," *Political Science Quarterly*, 68 (1953), 558. Reprinted in No. 2 above.

113. McClelland, Charles. "Applications of a general system theory in international relations," *Main Currents in Modern Thought*, 12 (1955), 27.

114. McCloskey, Robert G. "American conservatism and the democratic tradition," *Review of Politics,* 12 (1951), 3.

115. Miller, Warren E. "The socio-economic analysis of political behavior," *Midwest Journal of Political Science,* 2 (1958), 239.

116. Monypenny, Phillip. "Political science and the study of groups: notes to guide a research project," *Western Political Quarterly,* 7 (1954), 183.

117. Nixon, Charles R. "Freedom vs. unity: a problem in the theory of civil liberty," *Political Science Quarterly,* 68 (1953), 70.

118. Oppenheim, Felix E. "Control and unfreedom," *Philosophy of Science,* 22 (1955), 280.

119. Pennock, J. Roland. "The free speech doctrine: some doubts resolved," *Western Political Quarterly,* 3 (1950), 566.

120. Porter, John. "Elite groups: a scheme for the study of power in Canada," *Canadian Journal of Economics and Political Science,* 21 (1955), 498.

121. Pratt, R. C. "A note on David Easton's approach to political philosophy," *Canadian Journal of Economics and Political Science,* 20 (1954), 371.

122. Riemer, Neal. "The case for bare majority rule," *Ethics,* 62 (1951), 16.

123. Sabine, George H. "The two democratic traditions," *Philosophical Review,* 61 (1952), 451.

124. Schermerhorn, R. A. "Power as a primary concept in the study of minorities," *Social Forces,* 35 (1956), 53.

125. Sprout, Harold, and Sprout, Margaret. "Environmental factors in the study of international politics," *Conflict Resolution,* I (1957), 309.

126. Strauss, Leo. "On Locke's doctrine of natural rights," *Philosophical Review,* 41 (1952), 475.

127. Waldo, Dwight. "Administrative theory in the United States: a survey and prospect," *Political Studies,* 2 (1954), 70.

128. Wallace, Schuyler C. "Nullification: a process of government," *Political Science Quarterly,* 45 (1930), 347.

129. White, Howard B. "Edmund Burke on political theory and practice," *Social Research,* 17 (1950), 106.

VI. SELECTED READINGS ON POLITICAL SCIENCE AS DISCIPLINE AND PROFESSION

A. Books and Pamphlets

American Political Science Association, Committee for the Advancement of Teaching. *Goals for Political Science.* New York: Sloane, 1951.

——, Committee on Instruction. *The Teaching of Government.* New York: Macmillan, 1916.

——, Committee on Policy. *Report.* Supplement to *American Political Science Review,* 24 (March, 1930).

Anderson, William, and Gaus, John M. *Research in Public Administration.* Chicago: Public Administration Service, 1945.

Barker, Ernest. *The Study of Political Science and Its Relation to Cognate Fields.* Cambridge: Cambridge University, 1928.

Barnes, Harry Elmer (ed.). *The History and Prospects of the Social Sciences.* New York: Knopf, 1925.

Beard, Charles A. *The Nature of the Social Sciences.* New York: Charles Scribner's Sons, 1934. Chapter 3.

Berger, Morroe, and others (eds.). *Freedom and Control in Modern Society.* New York: Van Nostrand, 1954. Essay by George Catlin.

Brane, Dennis D. *A Sequential Science of Government: A Study in Systematic Political Science.* Cleveland: Western Reserve University, 1934.

Catlin, George E. G. *A Study of the Principles of Politics.* New York: Macmillan, 1930.

——. *The Science and Method of Politics.* New York: Knopf, 1927.

Contemporary Political Science. Cited above as No. 1.

de Grazia, Alfred. *The Elements of Political Science.* New York: Knopf, 1952. Chapter 1.

Easton, David. *The Political System: An Inquiry into the State of Political Science.* New York: Knopf, 1953.

Esslinger, William. *Politics and Science.* New York: Philosophical Library, 1955.

Field, Oliver P. *Political Science at Indiana University, 1829–1951.* Bloomington: Department of Government, Indiana University, 1952.

Griffith, Ernest S. (ed.). *Research in Political Science.* Chapel Hill, N.C.: University of North Carolina Press, 1948.

Hadow, Anna. *Political Science in American Colleges and Universities, 1636–1900.* New York: Appleton-Century, 1939.

Hallowell, John. *Religious Perspectives of College Teaching in Political Science.* New Haven: Edward W. Hazen Foundation, no date.

Harriman, Philip L., Roucek, Joseph S., and de Huszar, George B. (eds.). *Contemporary Social Science.* 2 vols. Harrisburg, Pa.: Stackpole, 1953. Essay in Vol. 1 by Joseph S. Roucek and Robert L. Chason.

Lasswell, Harold D. *Politics: Who Gets What, When, How.* New York: Whittlesey House, 1936.

———. *The Analysis of Political Behavior.* London: K. Paul, 1949.

Merriam, Charles E. *New Aspects of Politics.* Chicago: University of Chicago Press, 1931.

Ogburn, William F., and Goldenweiser, Alexander (eds.). *The Social Sciences and Their Interrelations.* Boston: Houghton Mifflin, 1927. Six chapters on political science.

Pollock, Frederick. *An Introduction to the History of the Science of Politics.* London: Macmillan, 1893.

Rankin, Robert S. *Political Science in the South.* University, Ala.: University of Alabama, 1946.

Ranney, Austin. *The Governing of Men.* New York: Henry Holt, 1958. Chapter 24.

Recent Developments in the Social Sciences. Philadelphia: Lippincott, 1927. Chapter by Charles E. Merriam.

Research Frontiers in Politics and Government. Cited above as No. 4.

Robson, William A. *The University Teaching of Social Sciences: Political Science.* Paris: UNESCO, 1954.

Rodee, Carlton C., Anderson, Totton J., and Christol, Carl Q. *Introduction to Political Science.* New York: McGraw-Hill, 1957. Chapter 1.

Shaw, George Bernard. *The Future of Political Science in America.* New York: Dodd, Mead, 1933.

Southern Political Science Association, Committee on Research. *Research Public Service and the Political Scientist in the South.* University, Ala.: University of Alabama, 1943.

Teaching of the Social Sciences. Paris: UNESCO, 1954. Chapter by Marshall E. Dimock on the teaching of political science.

Voegelin, Eric. *The New Science of Politics: An Introduction.* Chicago: University of Chicago Press, 1952.

Waldo, Dwight. *Political Science in the United States of America.* Paris: UNESCO, Documentation in the Social Sciences, 1956.

Wright, Quincy. *The Study of International Relations.* New York: Appleton-Century-Crofts, 1955.

Young, Roland (ed.). *Approaches to the Study of Politics.* Cited above as No. 8.

B. Articles

Agger, Robert E. "The social sciences in the study of politics," *Journal of Politics,* 18 (1956), 547.

American Political Science Association, Committee on War-time Services. "The political scientist and national service in war-time," *American Political Science Review,* 36 (1942), 931.

Anderson, William. "The role of political science," *American Political Science Review,* 37 (1943), 1.

——. "Political science North and South," *Journal of Politics,* 11 (1949), 298.

Appleby, Paul. "Political science: the next twenty-five years," *American Political Science Review,* 44 (1950), 924.

Beard, Charles A. "Neglected aspects of political science," *American Political Science Review,* 42 (1948), 211.

Catlin, George E. G. Cited above as No. 103.

Cook, Thomas I. "Politics, sociology, and values," *Journal of Social Philosophy*, 6 (1940), 35.

———. "The prospects of political science," *Journal of Politics*, 17 (1955), 265.

———. Cited above as No. 104.

Corwin, Edward S. "The democratic dogma and the future of political science," *American Political Science Review*, 23 (1929), 569.

Crick, Bernard. "The science of politics in the United States," *Canadian Journal of Economics and Political Science*, 20 (1954), 308.

Driscoll, Jean M., and Hyneman, Charles S. "Methodology for political scientists: perspectives for study," *American Political Science Review*, 49 (1955), 192. Reprinted in No. 2 cited above.

Eckstein, Harry. Cited above as No. 17.

Fairman, Charles. "The estate of political science," *Western Political Quarterly*, 1 (1948), 1.

Friedrich, Carl J. "Political science in the United States in wartime," *American Political Science Review*, 41 (1947), 978.

Garfinkel, Herbert, and Tierney, James F. "A coordinating course in the political science major," *American Political Science Review*, 51 (1957), 1178.

Gaus, John. "Job analysis of political science," *American Political Science Review*, 40 (1946), 217.

Hallowell, John. "Politics and ethics," *American Political Science Review*, 38 (1944), 639.

Hawley, Claude E., and Dexter, Lewis. "Recent political science research in American universities," *American Political Science Review*, 46 (1952), 470.

Heller, Hermann. "Political science," *Encyclopaedia of Social Sciences* (XII), 207–23.

Herring, Pendleton. "Political science in the next decade," *American Political Science Review*, 39 (1945), 757.

———. "On the study of government," *American Political Science Review*, 47 (1953), 961.

Kaufmann, Felix. "The issue of ethical neutrality in political science," *Social Research*, 16 (1949), 344.

Kelsen, Hans. "Science and politics," *American Political Science Review*, 45 (1951), 641.

Lasswell, Harold D. Cited above as Nos. 35 and 36.

Laves, Walter H. C. "The next decade in political science teaching," *American Political Science Review*, 34 (1940), 983.

Lindblom, Charles E. "In praise of political science," *World Politics*, 9 (1957), 240.

Lippincott, Benjamin E. Cited above as No. 77.

Macpherson, C. B. Cited above as No. 38.

Martin, Roscoe C. "Political science and public administration; a note on the state of the union," *American Political Science Review*, 46 (1952), 660.

Merriam, Charles E. "The present state of the study of politics," *American Political Science Review*, 15 (1921), 173.

Odegard, Peter H. "The political scientist in the democratic service state," *Journal of Politics*, 2 (1940), 140.

———. "Variations on a familiar theme," *American Political Science Review*, 45 (1951), 961.

Ogg, Frederic A. "Political science as a profession: from the standpoint of teaching," *Journal of Politics*, 3 (1941), 509.

Pennock, J. Roland. "Political science and political philosophy," *American Political Science Review*, 45 (1951), 1081.

Perry, Charner. "The semantics of political science," *American Political Science Review*, 44 (1950), 394. Followed by discussion by Herbert A. Simon, Max Radin, George A. Lundberg, and Harold D. Lasswell.

———. "Relations between ethics and politics," *Ethics*, 47 (1947), 163.

"Politics and ethics—a symposium," *American Political Science Review*, 40 (1946), 283. Essays by Gabriel Almond, Lewis Dexter, William Whyte, and John Hallowell.

Pollock, James K. "The primacy of politics," *American Political Science Review*, 45 (1951), 1.

Pound, Merritt B. "The Southern Political Science Association: an inventory," *Journal of Politics,* 11 (1949), 285.

"Research in political theory: a symposium," *American Political Science Review,* 38 (1944), 726. Essays by Francis G. Wilson, Benjamin F. Wright, Ernest S. Griffith, and Eric Voegelin.

Rockwell, Landon G. Cited above as No. 50.

Rossiter, Clinton. "Political Science I and political indoctrination," *American Political Science Review,* 52 (1948), 542.

Sabine, George H. "The pragmatic approach to politics," *American Political Science Review,* 24 (1932), 865.

Shannon, Jasper B. "An obituary of a political scientist," *Journal of Politics,* 13 (1951), 3.

Shipman, George A. "Research and public action," *Journal of Politics,* 1 (1939), 76.

Smith, Munro. "The domain of political science," *Political Science Quarterly,* 1 (1886), 1.

Spengler, J. J. "Generalists versus specialists in social science: an economist's view," *American Political Science Review,* 44 (1950), 358. Followed by discussion by Stuart A. Rice, Francis G. Wilson, and Thomas I. Cook.

Symposium, "Goals for political science: a discussion," *American Political Science Review,* 45 (1951), 996, and 46 (1952), 504. Eleven contributors.

Symposium, "Undergraduate instruction in political science," *American Political Science Review,* 41 (1947), 489. Essays by Francis O. Wilcox, Harvey C. Mansfield, James W. Fesler, John D. Millett, and Ethan P. Allen.

White, Leonard D. Cited above as No. 89.

Whyte, William F. "A challenge to political scientists," *American Political Science Review,* 37 (1943), 692.

Willoughby, William F. "A program for research in political science," *American Political Science Review,* 27 (1933), 1.

Wright, Quincy. "Political science and world stabilization," *American Political Science Review,* 44 (1950), 1.

INDEX